STELLAR CUSTOMER SERVICE

PRYOR Learning™

STELLAR CUSTOMER SERVICE

HOW TO KEEP THEM COMING BACK FOR MORE

& MEDIA

& MEDIA

Published 2025 by Gildan Media LLC
aka G&D Media
www.GandDmedia.com

Front cover design by David Rheinhardt of Pyrographx

Interior design by Meghan Day Healey of Story Horse, LLC

Library of Congress Cataloging-in-Publication Data is available upon request

ISBN: 978-1-7225-0730-5

10   9   8   7   6   5   4   3   2   1

CONTENTS

FOREWORD

Pryor Learning has been at the forefront of corporate train-ing, shaping the skills and careers of millions. Founded more than fifty years ago, when Fred Pryor pioneered the "One-day Seminar," Pryor Learning has become one of the nation's leading training providers, offering efficient, affordable, accessible career education for business profession-als. Our diverse offerings cater to a wide array of individuals and organizations alike, from small and mid-sized businesses to governments, nonprofits, and Fortune 500 companies.

Offering thousands of in-person seminars annually, Pryor Learning is synonymous with practical, hands-on training that delivers results. As the workforce continues to evolve, so do we—embracing new technologies and expanding our reach. Today, we offer a vast array of training options including in-person, live virtual, and on-demand formats, all designed to meet the diverse needs of a constantly changing workplace.

This book, and the series it belongs to, represents the next step in our mission to empower professionals with the essential skills they need to excel. In response to the growing popularity of eBooks and audiobooks, we aim to reach a new generation of learners, equipping them with the tools and knowledge to thrive in their careers. Our goal remains simple: to uphold Fred Pryor's legacy by making high-quality business training accessible to all, regardless of where they are in their career journey.

Join us in a tradition of learning that spans more than fifty years—a tradition that has empowered millions to achieve their professional goals. We invite you to explore the wealth of knowledge contained within these pages, knowing that you are part of something greater—a community dedicated to continuous growth and improvement. Welcome to Pryor Learning, where your success is our mission.

In today's competitive, customer-driven world, success isn't just about delivering products or services; it's about building lasting relationships. *Stellar Customer Service: How to Keep Them Coming Back for More* is your ultimate guide to transforming everyday interactions into memorable customer experiences. Packed with practical insights and proven strategies, this book equips you to go beyond meeting expectations, instead creating loyal advocates who keep coming back.

With *Stellar Customer Service,* you'll gain the skills to master every aspect of exceptional customer care. From active listening and empathetic communication to navigating challenging situations with confidence, each chapter builds your expertise. You'll learn how to optimize live chat and email interactions for maximum impact, balancing personalization with efficiency. For team leaders, this book provides valuable techniques to inspire and support high-performing teams. Whether you're on the front line or managing a service team, this guide provides you with practical tips and information to deliver remarkable experiences that drive loyalty and success.

ONE

The Elements of Customer Service

ere's a quick overview of the topics we'll be covering in this chapter:

1. The most important employees in an organization, from the standpoint both of the organization and the customer.

2. Keeping emotions at bay. That's really hard sometimes. We'll go over some tips and tricks for keeping keep emotions at bay, for you and the customer.

3. Giving the customer what they want. This is a critical element of customer service. We need to make our customers happy to make sure they continue to use our business.

4. Tips for sticky situations. Every employee who has a public interface has encountered a difficult customer. We'll talk about some tips for handling those customers professionally.

5. After the encounter: An important item of customer service is follow-up, keeping customers happy and main-

taining contact to make sure that they continue using our business.

The Most Important Employees

Who do you think are the most important employees in an organization? Go ahead, take a guess.

According to most organizational charts, the CEO, the chief executive officer, is the most important employee in an organization, followed by upper management, then middle management, then the direct supervisors. The frontline employees are at the bottom of the totem pole.

But from a customer standpoint, it's just the opposite. Frontline employees are the most important. They can either keep a customer happy or turn them away from doing business with the company. They make the business successful for the CEO and upper management.

Here's one story: a woman bought some sheets in a comforter set. When she got them home, she found that they had been used. She was livid, ready to go in and let that company have it. She marched back into the store, went to the customer service desk, and of course dealt with a frontline employee. The customer explained her situation and how angry and upset she was.

The young lady behind the desk said, "Well, dang, I would be mad too."

What do you think that did for the customer? First of all, it took the wind out of her sails. Her anger dissipated, and she ended up laughing with the young lady behind the customer service desk.

That is a great example of how a frontline employee is the most important employee in an organization. The customer ended up having a great experience with that company—because of the frontline employee, not the CEO or upper management.

Frontline employees give the customer a positive or negative impression of the company.

By the way, that customer told her story to twenty people at a dinner party. Those people all retold the story, so in the end, hundreds of people are going to hear positive comments about that company—because of one great customer service representative.

><><><><><><><><><><><><><><><><><><><><><><><><><><><><><><><><><><><>

The customer service representative is the most important person in the company.

><><><><><><><><><><><><><><><><><><><><><><><><><><><><><><><><><><><>

What We Can't Control

Let's focus on some things that we can't control at our company. Why would we want to do that? Why do we want to start off talking about customer complaints by saying what we can't control?

We need to recognize the things we can't control: things or situations that are out of our authority. We don't control corporate policy. A company's policies are written. We follow them, understand them, enforce them, but we can't control them. Of course, we can always give ideas and suggestions. We can pass on information to our managers. But as customer service representatives, we can't control corpo-rate policy.

Next, we can't control what someone else told a customer about our company. If I'm picking up the phone with an angry customer and I'm the fourth representative they've talked to, they're going to be swayed, persuaded, angry, or upset based on what the previous three people have said to them and how they've been treated by those employees. We can't control that. You can't control what someone else told them about your company before you pick up their call.

Next item: product quality. Hopefully, you work for compa-nies whose product quality is high. Nonetheless, as customer service reps, we cannot control product quality—certainly not on the spot.

The next item is pricing. Pricing is not set by frontline employees. Most of the time, pricing is out of our control. We can explain it or justify it, but normally we can't change it.

Finally, we can't control how the customer acts. When they call in, they may be in a good mood or a bad mood. We have no control over their emotions on the other end of the line. One employee who was working on Christmas Eve had a phone call. The gentleman on the other end immedi-ately started yelling at the employee before even giving her a chance to ask if she could help. He was irate, rude, and extremely upset, but the employee realized that his behavior may have had to do with the fact that it was Christmas Eve. She listened for a while, remaining calm and asking questions when appropriate. She let him rant and rave for a while. By the end of that conversation (which by the way did take quite some time), the customer was happy and satisfied. He even wrote a letter about the employee's customer service to upper management.

Put yourself in the other person's shoes. When a customer calls in, we can't control how they act. However, listening is a skill that we should put up front when a customer calls.

><><><><><><><><><><><><><><><><><><><><><><><><><><><><><><><><><><><><><><><><

We can't control how a customer acts. But listening is a skill we should put up front when a customer calls.

><><><><><><><><><><><><><><><><><><><><><><><><><><><><><><><><><><><><><><><><

What We *Can* Control

Let's move on and talk about some ways we can take care of what we *can* control. What can we control as frontline employees, as customer service representatives? First of all, we can control our attitude: we can have a positive attitude. Whether we're meeting the customer face-to-face or over the phone, they will pick up on our attitude immediately. So have a positive attitude about your company and your job and about being a great customer service representative.

We can also control our own emotions, even if a customer is angry and upset, as we saw with the story about the gentleman on Christmas Eve. We don't have to be angry and upset; we control our emotions and our response.

As mentioned above, active listening is an important element of resolving customer complaints on the spot. Listen to your customers and respond appropriately. Sometimes no response is needed. Sometimes they just need to talk about how upset they are and they talk themselves right out of being upset.

Follow your company policy and respond appropriately. Control your attitude, emotions, and response.

The 7/11 Rule

Let's talk for a few minutes about the 7/11 rule: In the first 7 seconds of contact with your customer, they form 11 impressions about you and your company. What do those 11 first impressions have to do with?

In the first 7 seconds of contact with your customer, they form 11 impressions about you and your company.

Cleanliness. The cleanliness of your organization, your office area, and you (your uniform, for example).

Attractiveness. This doesn't mean physical beauty; it has to do with the attractiveness of your office area. Is it clean and neat? Is your own appearance clean, neat, and attractive?

Credibility. Can the customer believe you? Do they have confidence in your credibility? This goes hand in hand with knowledge. Are you knowledgeable about the company's product, pricing, structure, and responsiveness? Customers want quick responses. Always try to respond to a customer within the first ten seconds if at all possible.

Friendliness. A smile is a smile universally. Everyone understands a smile, no matter what language you speak. Friendliness is one of the biggest first impressions that your customer will get from your company. Practice smiling.

Helpfulness. Are you truly willing to help the customer? Do you have their best interests at heart? Are you willing to go out of your way? If you work in a retail store and someone asks the location of an item, if at all possible, escort them to see that item. If you're a customer service representative and you work on the phone, show a willingness to help and communicate that. Say, "I'll be more than happy to help you with that issue."

Courtesy. Be courteous. Use expressions that we all learned at school: *please*; *thank you*; *yes, sir*; and *yes, ma'am*.

Have confidence. This should be instilled in you from upper management. Have confidence in your decisions. Use a voice tone that shows confidence and professionalism. Be professional.

Managing Emotions

Whether you're on the phone with a customer or face-to-face, we all deal with angry customers at some point. As customer service representatives, our goal is to stay calm even when the other person is not.

◇◇

We all deal with angry customers at some point.

◇◇

Here's a fact to help you keep emotions at bay: 85 percent of your behavior comes from what you think about yourself, your self-esteem, and your self-confidence. Know that you're unique and you're valuable to your organization.

On the other hand, 15 percent of your behavior comes from reacting to someone else's words and actions. It's very easy for that to kick in sometimes. When someone is yelling at you and criticizing you based on your organization's behavior, pricing, or beliefs, it's sometimes easy to take that personally.

Remember that this is not personal. The customer on the other end of the line is not attacking you personally (although it may feel as if they are). One way to keep emotions at bay is to remember that you are unique, you are valuable, and you contribute a tremendous amount of value to your organization.

Quit taking it personally. Here's an idea for you: whenever you feel like you're being attacked personally at your job, visualize a Q-tip, the Q standing for *Quit taking it personally.* Stay calm, talk in a calm voice and keep thinking to yourself: *Q-tip, Q-tip, Q-tip.* Quit taking it personally.

◇◇

Quit taking it personally

◇◇

The ABC Theory

Let's talk about Albert Ellis's ABC theory of emotional disturbance, which posits that an activating event (A) leads to an emotional consequence (C) based on one's irrational beliefs (B) about that event.

Here's a personal story. Casey is a relationship banker and as such gets a lot of yelling from customers. When she started her job, she thought, am I doing something wrong? Why are they so upset with me? Several days in a row, she went home from work feeling very depressed and upset, wondering that maybe she wasn't doing her job well.

Let's look at this experience in the light of the ABC theory. In two out of the three cases, customers had overdrawn their accounts, which had been closed by the bank. In these cases, the activating experience (A) was a customer who was extremely angry. Casey had an incorrect belief (B) that she wasn't doing her job right. This led to an emotional consequence (C) of being upset. But in fact, the closed account was the customer's problem, not Casey's. Once she realized this, she could stop being upset.

When someone asks you a question and they're upset because of your answer, ask, am I being rational in what I believe here? Is this my fault? What emotional consequence am I having based on this conversation? Should I be depressed? Should I be angry? Should I be upset, or is this just a part of my job?

Let's add a D and E to the ABC theory. D: *dispute* irrational ideas. Often when we're dealing with angry customers and are trying to keep our emotions at bay, it's irrational to think that this is our fault. In some cases, we may be dealing with misdirected anger. As we've already seen, we cannot control what other people have told this customer prior to our phone call. We might be dealing with misdirected anger based on the customer's previous service experience. Then E: choose a new *effect*.

We'll wrap this together with our 85 percent and 15 percent rule: 85 percent of the way we react comes from the way we feel about ourselves. We need to have high self-esteem and self-confidence. Remember that you are unique and valuable to your organization, and choose a new effect. Don't let an irrational belief convince you that you're not doing your job well.

If you're faced with an issue about your job performance, ask a question. For example, your boss says, "I'm not happy with this work." That would be A: the activating experience. You could jump to B, an irrational belief, and think, "Oh my goodness, I'm not good at my job; I can't do anything right." Instead, you can take a step back and say, "I understand you're not happy with that work. Let's work together. What can I do differently to have a better experience for both of us in the future?" Choose a new effect: E.

Here are a few attitudes and actions that can anger a customer:

- Arguing
- Rationalizing
- Defending
- Complaining
- Overreacting
- Emotionalizing

- Overpromising
- Guaranteeing
- Judging

Now here are some winning attitudes:
- A professional and polite demeanor. This does not mean a canned response. Customers will pick up on any canned response that you've been forced to say.
- A "how can I help?" attitude, with emphasis on the word *can*. Have an attitude of wanting to help your customer.
- Be sincere; be honest; use integrity.
- Empathy. Everyone has a story, and there are two sides to every story. Try to put yourself in the other person's shoes.
- Listen. Listening to customers is one of the most important aspects of resolving complaints on the spot. We all should have active listening as one of our goals. Use your body language and your words to show that you are actively listening.
- Underpromise and overdeliver: always a great idea when resolving customer complaints. Surprise your customer: overdeliver; go above and beyond normal customer service if at all possible. Keep your company policy in mind, follow the rules, and do everything that you can to go above and beyond.

Underpromise and overdeliver.

- Take ownership of the problem. There's nothing more frustrating than dealing with someone who constantly says, "It's not my problem; I didn't do that; I can't fix that." Here are some words to avoid when we're dealing with our customers: *I can't*; *all we can do is . . .* ; *it's company policy*; *you should have* or *shouldn't have.*
- Pay attention to your tone of voice and your body language when dealing with customers. Words convey a great deal of information. but so do body language and tone.

Give the Customer What They Want

Most of the time, satisfying our customers is very simple and basic. When it comes to complaints, the first thing customers want is an apology: a very sincere, "I'm sorry." Then an explanation is necessary. Why did this happen? Help your customer understand what the problem is, and then confidently assure them that it will not happen again.

Let's dive a little bit deeper into each of these categories. In the first place, not all apologies are created equal. A flippant "I'm sorry" is very different than a genuine "I'm sorry that happened to you." A study done by the Nottingham School of Economics Center for Division Research said 40 percent of customers want an apology. Sometimes that's all that's necessary. When someone from the company sincerely says, "I'm sorry," customers are often satisfied, and it may not be necessary to take further steps, such as giving them a refund or a gift card.

Apologies are very powerful; use them. After all, don't you respect your coworkers and others in your life who admit they've made a mistake and say, "I'm sorry"? More importantly, they recognize the problem and come up with a solution: "I'm sorry, and here's what we can do to take care of that problem for you." We can listen to the customer and take responsibility for the issue they are having.

The next step in giving the customer what they want is an explanation. Give the facts, along with some advice, but keep it brief. They are probably not interested in the fact that your system may have been down for the last two weeks, and that's why they have an error on their billing statement. Instead of giving all those details—which the customer really isn't interested in—say, "I see the problem, and I'll fix it."

A third step for giving the customer what they want is to assure them this will not happen again. Back that up with a reason: "I apologize that your food did not come out the way you ordered it. Our kitchen has been having a little bit of an issue, and I assure you that the next time you visit our restaurant, this will not happen again." Assure the customer that you are following up and trying your best to handle this situation.

Now let's talk about a situation where you may not be able to promise the customer that this will not happen again. Let's say this is an issue that happens frequently at your company, and management doesn't seem to be responding adequately. At this point, tell the customer you understand the problem, apologize, explain it, and assure them that you are following up and letting management know about the issue. Brief facts, honesty, and sincerity—all of those things go hand in hand to let your customer know you are following up; you are listening to what they are saying. The customer knows you will follow up with the problem to help ensure that it will not happen again.

Let's review the basics of giving the customer what they want: the apology, the explanation, and the assurance that this will not happen again. Recently a woman went into her favorite coffee shop. It was a busy morning, and she did not get her coffee in time. She stood and stood while six other people who were behind her got their coffees. As soon as the barista recognized the situation, he said, "It seems that you've been standing there a while; did we miss your order?"

"Yes. Here's my order; here's the drink that I want."

He explained that the order did not move from the cashier to the barista. He apologized. He made the drink quickly and handed it to the customer with a gift card for a free drink next time.

Everyone makes mistakes. No one is perfect. Getting that apology—a brief, five-second explanation assuring the customer the barista would do his best to keep this from happening again and handing her a free gift card for the next coffee—was imperative; it was critical to keep that customer, who walked away very happy.

We've already talked about putting yourself in the other person's shoes. When you are the customer, the customer service rep is on the other side of the counter. Put yourself in their shoes. We all know how they feel. One lady was at a fast-food restaurant a few months ago. The person in front of her was irate because their order had come out incorrectly. The young lady behind the counter did exactly what she was supposed to do: she apologized, she explained the situation, she tried to give free food, and she apologized again. For some reason, the lady in line must have had some misdirected anger, because she continued to berate the customer service representative for at least three minutes until the young lady cried.

◇◇

Put yourself in the other person's shoes.

◇◇

At that point, a manager from the back of the store came out and took care of the customer. However, the young lady who did her best to follow these steps, apologized, and tried to make the customer happy walked away in tears.

When we're on the other side of the counter or the other end of the phone, keep in mind the customer service rep that we're dealing with has the same problems and issues that we have. Put yourself in their shoes.

Resolving Complaints

Let's establish a framework for resolving a complaint. Of course, we'll never get two complaints that are the same, if only because we'll never have two customers that are the same. However, we do know that as customer service representatives, *we* will have problems. We *will* deal with angry customers. Part of resolving customer issues on the spot is adhering to this framework:

First, determine the problem. The best way to do that is to listen to the customer. Listen to what they're saying. Listen to the problem they are describing, and then repeat the problem back for confirmation. Use the words they used rather than restating their problem in your own language. Be careful: if you parrot their words straight back to them word for word, it could make them angry. But repeat the problem, make sure you've understood it correctly, and then thank them and apologize.

Next, sincerely thank the customer for bringing the problem to your attention. Sometimes when they bring a problem to our attention, it's good for our company. It's an issue that we can resolve before many more customers have the same complaint.

Then seek the best solution. As a customer service representative, you may be able to offer several solutions. If none of the solutions you offer work for this customer, ask what would make them happy. When you use your best judgment while following your company policy, you and the customer can agree on the best solution.

Finally, take quick action. Nothing frustrates a customer more than having someone assure them that they will follow up, but nothing happens: a week later, the customer has to make another phone call. They're getting angrier and more upset now because someone promised them that they would follow up with the problem but did not. When you're presented with a problem, take quick action, follow up, and let the customer know that the issue has been resolved.

Sticky Situations

As customer service representatives, we're going to have to deal with sticky situations.

One of the most difficult situations is having to say no to our customer. We want to say yes, but sometimes we just have to say no. If the customer's request is totally unreasonable, we'll have to tell that customer, "No, we are not able to do that." Here's how to soften that response. Again, actively listen. Active listening is a huge part of resolving customer complaints on the spot. Listen to what the customer's saying, acknowledge what they're saying, repeat what you hear them say, and then sincerely decline their request.

Here's one example. One couple has a vacation rental home, which they rent out by the week. One time the guests had to leave for a few days because of a water leak. The owners acknowledged the guests' disappointment and gave them their money back immediately. But the guests requested both to stay in the house and to get their money back. That wasn't a good solution because the repairs couldn't be done with the guests in the house.

Although the owners wanted to make the guests happy, they did have to decline. They did so by acknowledging the guests' disappointment, saying they were sincerely sorry that the guests had to leave for a couple days and stay in a hotel, then politely explaining that it would not work for them to be in the home while the repairs were being made.

A great way to end conversations when you're negotiating with a customer and you have to tell them no is to say, "Would that be fair?" Asking the question in this manner focuses on your solution. The customer thinks about the solution you're offering rather than other things they may want.

Another situation that we often encounter is the broken record: the customer who continues to complain about the same thing over and over. The way to handle that is to be empathetic, show concern in our voice, and offer our solution. When the broken-record customer comes back and complains about the same problem again and again, we want to continually offer our solution. Try to use the same words and phrases as you repeat the solution over and over. This customer is probably trying to get you to give in, thinking the more he complains, the more likely you are to give in.

Follow your company policy and continue to state that policy in a professional and tactful manner. Be courteous, have a good attitude, have a good tone in your voice, and repeat the company policy back to the broken-record customer. Eventually you should come to an agreement.

How do you handle the customer who demands to speak to the boss? The first approach is to say, "For reasons of privacy, I can't transfer you directly to my supervisor, but I can give you their voicemail. Is that acceptable?"

Make sure you find out and follow your company guidelines for handling a customer who demands to speak to the boss. Know beforehand whom you should pass these complaints to. A nice way to pass along a customer who demands to speak to the boss is to stay on the phone and make sure they get to the supervisor. It's called a *soft transfer*. Stay on the phone with the customer. When the supervisor answers, provide a brief overview of the customer's situation. This shows a caring attitude on your part. Sometimes when you pass a customer along to a supervisor, the rules will be overridden. In that case, ask your boss how you should handle this situation in the future.

What are we going to do with the angry, exploding customer? This is the person who is beyond upset. They're yelling and screaming, potentially using foul language.

First, acknowledge their emotions. Back to active listening: listen to their complaint; acknowledge their emotions. You can use phrases like "I understand," "I hear what you're saying," "I see your point." Then try to move the conversation on; try to resolve the issue by saying, "This is as important to me as it is to you. I am committed and dedicated to solving this problem. I see that you're upset. It's important to me to solve this too."

By the way, is it OK to vent sometimes? Yes, of course it is. It's OK to vent. We all do it at some point. Allow your angry customer to vent. Set a time limit to yourself—maybe thirty or forty-five seconds—and then move the conversation along. You can do that by interrupting and saying, "I understand you're upset. It's important to me to resolve this issue also."

As for the customer who is using foul language, one way to handle them is to politely interrupt and explain that you're really struggling to hear their complaint but that you are offended by the foul language. Emphasize that you want to help, be empathetic, and listen, but do not allow the language to continue.

Emphasize that you want to help, be empathetic, and listen, but do not allow foul language to continue.

In short, with angry customers, acknowledge the anger. You can do that by looking directly at your customer, if it's a face-to-face situation, and saying, "I understand. I can see that you are very upset." Acknowledge their anger. Allow them to vent, but set a time limit. Allow them to vent for a specified time, but don't let them cross the line of emotional abuse; don't let them use four-letter words. Put a stop to that quickly.

Another suggestion is to remove barriers. What does that mean? If you're behind a big mahogany desk, stand up and walk to the front of the desk. If your customer's standing, try to stand. If your customer's sitting, try to sit. Studies have proven that people emulate our behavior. If you speak in a calm tone, more than likely your customer will also begin to speak in a calm tone.

Keep a close eye on your body language. Make sure your arms aren't crossed when you're listening to your customer. Make sure you have an open posture. Smiling is always a good idea. Make eye contact when appropriate. Use your body language and remove barriers to assure your customer that you are actively listening.

Make sure you know your company policy on violence. What does your policy say regarding customer behavior? What defines crossing the line? Hopefully, for your benefit as a frontline employee, whenever your safety feels threat-ened, you should be able to call security; you should be able to get yourself out of that situation. Speak with your manag-ers about company policy. Know and understand what limits can be pushed. Managers, encourage your employees to ask for help when necessary. When a frontline employee is able to get a manager and the manager walks in with a bit more authority and uses stronger body language, that will calm the customer. Managers, make sure you always support your frontline employees. They too take a lot of complaints and sometimes abuse from customers.

After you've encountered a situation like this, take a time-out. Take a break; walk around the block if possible. If nothing else, go to the break room and take a few deep breaths.

How to Handle Sticky Situations

- Be a Q-tip. Don't take it personally.
- Try to use sense of humor when possible.
- Remember that in any threatening situation, you can call security, or you can call the police.
- Know your company policy.
- If the same sticky situation continues to happen, ask, "What steps can I take? What steps can my company take to avoid this situation?"

If the same sticky situation continues to happen, ask, "What steps can I take? What steps can my company take to avoid this situation?" If there's a problem with the process or the product, frontline employees will be the first ones to recognize it. Point those out. Maybe you could bring the issue up at a staff meeting; maybe you can communicate it via email. During your staff meeting, ask others if they're having the same sticky situation, if they're encountering the same problems over and over. Dive deeper into that situation so that you can get rid of it and move forward.

Learn from every complaint. It's natural to become defensive when we're being criticized or when people are complaining. Take a step back, take a deep breath, and realize what you can learn from this complaint. Brainstorm with your team. How can we learn from this mistake? In today's world, with social media, it's incredibly important to learn what we did wrong, fix it, and move forward. Studies have shown that the biggest reason customers quit a business is indifference from the manager or frontline employees. Show an attitude of active listening, empathy, and caring. Learn from every complaint, and then fix the problem that was pointed out.

Sometimes customers are our greatest resource for fixing our systems. In one company that sold weather data, one of the systems had a small error. A subset of customers who served as testers found an error in one program. Fortunately, this was a small subset of customers, enabling the company to fix the system immediately and without widespread complaints.

We spoke earlier about thanking your customer. We apologize, we acknowledge, and then we thank them for finding problems and helping us come to solutions. The customer feels empowered and appreciated. It's a great way to resolve customer complaints on the spot.

It's also a good idea to pay attention to procedures. When someone demands to speak to the boss, for example, how is that handled? How is that procedure handled in your area? As you move forward to dealing with complaints, analyze how well or how poorly each complaint was handled and resolved. Bring your team together using a brainstorming session. Make it a goal to analyze how well or how poorly the complaint was handled and resolved.

What's a brainstorming session? Everyone gets in the room and throws out ideas to evaluate a situation. No idea, thought, or sentence is criticized. The ideas are all assembled and taken down to be evaluated in another meeting. (We'll go more into brainstorming in chapter 5.)

Debriefing Sessions

Debriefing sessions can be extremely useful for handling and resolving complaints. Make sure to have different levels of management present. Frontline employees need to be there too. Many of the best suggestions come from frontline employees, who are dealing with customers and know how to resolve the problems. Most of the time, they know exactly what the customer wants. If we can also have a customer attend the debrief, that would be optimal.

Define the steps for the debrief. Set an agenda and send it out in advance so that everyone knows what to expect. Make sure everyone comes prepared for the debrief, and define the role for each participant. We also want to have someone who will take notes or serve as a scribe for the session. Make sure the notes are clear and concise and are distributed quickly. We don't want them to simply be typed up, sent out, and stuck in a drawer. We want to learn from this experience.

In the beginning of the meeting, remind everyone to be a Q-tip: don't take any of the comments personally. The purpose of the meeting is to determine what we've done well and what we need to improve, and move forward together.

We're all here in the debrief together to learn and help our company move forward.

Here are a few ideas and suggestions to help you get the debrief going: Start by focusing on the positive. The first question we can ask is, what have we learned from success? What was good about this customer complaint? How did we improve based on the input?

Then address what you've learned from the failure. Make sure to set it up so that everyone in the room knows it's OK to fail. We all mess up. Everyone messes up. What did we learn from this failure? How can we move forward? Failing forward is an option. We learn from our mistakes and move forward from there.

Then take this process to another level: what if we had done X? Again, allow employees, particularly frontline employees, to brainstorm. What if we had gone down a different path? What if we had chosen to do X or taken path Y? Think those through; talk out loud. In a brainstorming session, one idea sparks another. Once we start having these discussions, we'll be able to use others' ideas and input to move forward.

One extremely effective way to give feedback in a debriefing session is, first of all, to talk about what you liked best. What did we like best about the way we handled this customer complaint? Make sure to congratulate employees who are doing that well. Be specific and timely when giving that praise.

Then move to the next step: What do we want to do differently next time? How can we handle this better in the future? What should look different the next time we go through this situation? What should sound different? Give employees very clear input: here's the praise, here's what you did well, here's what I would like to see done differently next time.

The final step in the debrief should be recommendations for the future. Make sure everyone in the room is allowed to speak. What is my recommendation for how to handle this encounter in the future?

A debriefing session can be one hour, or four hours, depending on the nature of the customer complaint. If this is a complaint that comes up frequently, take a few steps back, sit down, and have a debriefing session. Spend enough time to think about how to move forward so that this customer complaint doesn't continually happen.

As an end result, develop recommendations for the future and present them to upper management so that your organization can move forward properly.

◇◇◇

Give everyone the chance to vent.

◇◇◇

Another piece of advice: when you start your debriefing session, allow everyone in the room time to vent. One manager does this brilliantly: in every debriefing session with him, he allows everyone in the room time to vent. He does this by asking open-ended questions. If you are the facilitator, give everyone in the room time to talk, and let them know it's OK to vent. Everyone might be on edge, especially if this is a customer complaint that happens often. Allow time to vent, and then cut it off. Be skilled in facilitating so that you know what time frame to allow so you'll be able to move on with the debrief. But it's critically important in the beginning to let everyone know that it's OK to be frustrated. Handling a customer complaint on the spot is frustrating. We can commiserate with each other, then we can move forward and talk about how to take care of the situation better next time.

Get Customer Feedback

Then ask customers for feedback. It's very easy in today's world to ask your customers for feedback. If you ordered an appliance last week from a major retail store, you're likely to get an email within an hour, asking, "Please provide feedback." Similarly, when you call an organization and speak with a customer service representative, immediately afterward you're likely to get an email asking for feedback,

One method used in fast-food and coffee chains is to say at the bottom of the receipt, "If you will answer this survey, you'll get a free coffee the next time you come in." In today's social media world, it's important for organizations to ask for feedback: many people will put feedback about a company on their social media pages.

We need to do everything possible to make sure the feedback is positive. Take criticism as an opportunity to make things better. This is hard. Most of us get defensive immediately. Understandably, handling emotions can be the hardest part of our job when we're resolving customer complaints on the spot. When someone yells, our natural reaction is to yell back.

A successful company takes criticism well. They take customer input and move forward with the ideas they get.

After the encounter, remember that a customer who comes back after a negative experience is a customer for life. They are committed to your organization. To go back to the story about the woman with the complaint about buying used sheets, although that was a negative experience, it was handled well. She had a very negative experience, but one customer service representative turned that around. She tells everyone the story because it's funny, and she is committed to that company for life. Keep that in mind. Follow up after the encounter. Make sure your customer is happy if at all possible.

A final note: the only person who can make you unhappy is you. As customer service representatives, we see and talk to people all the time, and sometimes we feel it's their goal just to make us unhappy. But always remember: the only person who can make you unhappy is you.

Key Points in This Chapter

1. The customer service representative is the most important person in the company.
2. Keep your emotions at bay.
3. Don't take negative reactions personally.
4. Give customers what they want.
5. Sometimes an apology is all the customer wants.
6. Follow up afterward to keep the customer in touch with your company.

TWO

Dealing with Difficult Customers

n this chapter, we'll share some techniques and advice for dealing with difficult customers that you encounter in your workplace. Of course, nothing in this chapter—or in this book—should be construed as legal advice. If you have legal questions, please consult an attorney.

No matter how good you are at your job, and no matter how much emphasis you place on outstanding service, if you deal with customers, you'll have to deal with difficult customer experiences. When customers are confrontational, overdemanding, or unreasonable, it becomes harder than ever to deliver helpful and courteous service.

But when customers are met with a take-charge attitude and a positive outlook, customers immediately feel good about doing business with your organization. In this chapter, we will explore not only how to deal with difficult customers and their complaints, but how to learn from them so that we can prevent future problems while solving the current ones.

We can start by understanding customers. What do they really want? When you can start to understand things from a customer's point of view, you can see how they might get difficult when they don't get what they want and expect.

Then we'll go a little bit more in depth in understanding what makes a customer difficult. Different people are difficult for different reasons. We will explore the most common types of difficult people, along with the techniques for handling each type.

Next, we'll take a look at the seven steps to dealing with difficult customers. This proven step-by-step process will help you have confidence in navigating this stressful experience. You will learn what it takes to turn the situation around and provide the kind of superior and memorable service that results in a satisfied, loyal customer.

We will then proceed to explore some additional tips for handling difficult customers that will help you personally stay focused, positive, and strong. They will enable you to easily move through the steps when dealing with customer complaints and upsets.

Then we'll finish up by giving you ways to prevent difficult customer situations before they even happen.

Understanding Customers

Several years ago, a JetBlue flight attendant had had enough of abuse from difficult customers. He used the airplane's public address system to tell off a rude passenger and announced that this was it. He was done. Then he activated the plane's inflatable emergency chute. He grabbed two beers and slid down onto the runway, quitting his job in a blaze of glory.

That flight attendant, Steven Slater, has become something of a hero to the everyday worker. He had had enough of dealing with difficult customers and was fed up enough to tell a customer what he really thought, then make his exit in the most dramatic way possible.

If you have ever dealt with a difficult customer, I'm sure there are times when you wish you could do the same thing. While I certainly understand Mr. Slater's frustration, dealing with customers—of all kinds—is a requirement of virtually any job in which an employee comes into direct contact with the public.

<<><><><><><><><><><><><><><><><><><><><><><><><><><><><><><><><><><>

**Dealing with customers—of all kinds—
is a requirement of virtually any job in which
an employee comes into public contact.**

<<><><><><><><><><><><><><><><><><><><><><><><><><><><><><><><><><><>

Being able to deal effectively with customers—even ones who might be difficult—and having employees who are able to do so as well is essential to a business's ability to operate. If you are a frontline employee, supervisor, or business owner and must deal with the members of the public, you are the face of the organization. You need to know how to, and be able to, act appropriately in challenging situations.

Difficult customers come in all shapes and sizes. They're difficult for several reasons. Can you think of a time when you yourself might have been seen as a difficult customer?

You probably can, even though you thought you were being perfectly reasonable at the time. The reason? In the end, it always comes down to the same thing: you didn't get what you thought you should be getting.

That is the one thing that all difficult customers have in common: they're not getting what they want or expect. No matter what you're selling, you're also selling customer satisfaction. A satisfied customer may tell a few people about their good experience, but a dissatisfied customer will tell many people.

Given the number of ways that people today have of sharing their bad experiences—through social media, for example—it's more important than ever to find the best way to give your customers a positive experience. The way to do that is to give them what they want.

So what do customers want? Since we have all been customers at one time or another, put yourself in your customer's place and think: "When I'm the customer, I want . . ." and then fill in the blank.

Whether you're running a small business or a large corporation, whether you're selling dollar store items or luxury products, every customer wants at least some of the same things. Let's look at a few of the top things that customers want. See if you don't agree that when you are the customer, you want these things too.

First, *respect*. No matter what type of service the customer is receiving—from the one who cuts their hair to the one who cuts their lawn, all customers want some degree of respect.

One man visited a restaurant recently in a high-rent district, so he expected a certain level of respect and service.

He arrived early and was meeting a colleague for a business meeting in between lunch and dinner, so the restaurant was relatively empty. The employees were all talking and laughing together at the back of the restaurant. The businessman was not greeted when he entered the restaurant. In fact, he was completely ignored. After waiting several minutes, he shouted out, "Should I go ahead and seat myself?" One of the employees, visibly annoyed by the interruption, finally approached the man, and without an apology, tried seating him near the restroom, even though the restaurant was nearly empty. The customer asked to sit in another location. The employee rolled their eyes and sat him where he requested.

The customer was now beyond the point of losing his patience, because he wasn't getting what he wanted or expected. After another ten minutes of being ignored by the waitstaff, without even water or a drink request, his colleague finally arrived. They promptly left the restaurant and dined elsewhere. Although this customer was very patient and forgiving, he felt so disrespected by the way he was treated that he wrote a scathing review on the Internet. Now he tells all his business associates to stay clear of that restaurant, and he will never return himself.

Customers want and expect that the person who is assisting them will focus on them and help them get what they want. Customers want to feel that you care about their needs. In this case, the waitstaff clearly did not provide that. The fact that there was no apology, along with the rolling of the eyes and no service, made this customer feel the waitstaff was ignoring him and did not care about his needs.

Customers want to feel that you care about their needs.

Customers want to feel that you care about their needs. If a customer has a problem, they want to know that you care and are invested in helping them solve that problem. They are not interested in excuses. How frustrating is it for you as a customer when you ask a question and you're told, "I don't know; it's not my job"? Customers are not interested in excuses, even if they're valid. They don't want to be told that the computer is down or that the shipment has been delayed or that your technician is out sick. They just want to hear what you can do to get the job done.

Customers want basic courtesies. They want a pleasant greeting and a good attitude. Would you return to a restaurant where they were annoyed to have to seat you? How much money would you spend in a store if the salesperson was rude every time you visited? Probably not much, if you even return in the first place.

Customers want fairness. How would it make you feel if you found out that another customer got a much better deal than you did for the same product or service?

Customers also want speed. They do not like to wait. Generally, the faster that you can deliver what the customer wants, the better their experience will be. Have you ever gone through an automated voice system, answering half a dozen questions, only to be sent to the wrong person, who puts you on hold for five minutes, then transfers you to yet another wrong person? Sometimes you can become a very difficult customer over very minor issues simply because you have spent half a day trying to get to the person who could finally answer your question.

Customers want honesty. If you fail to live up to your promises, not only will you have an unsatisfied customer on your hands, but they will spread the word about the broken promises to anyone who will listen. Most people aren't just shopping for a product or service; they're looking for a solution to their problem. If you can solve their issue and provide satisfaction, you have a happy customer.

◇◇◇

Most people aren't just shopping for a product or service; they're looking for a solution to their problem.

◇◇◇

Customers want you to be skilled. They look at you as the expert at your own job; that's part of what they're paying you for. One woman hired a virtual assistant who claimed that she had a lot of website and technical skills. But it took more time for the employer to train the assistant than it would have taken to do the job herself. The woman didn't get what she wanted and expected, so she never used the assistant's services again.

Customers want appreciation. They want to have a sense that their business is important to you. Who wants to spend money with someone that doesn't appreciate their business?

Customers want a product or service to be available. One mother was searching high and low for a specific toy for her daughter's birthday. It was the only thing her daughter wanted, and the mother was determined to find it. She called store after store until finally she found exactly what she was looking for at a store three hours away. The sales associate on the phone assured her that they would have the toy available and would put it on hold for her to pick up the next day. Excited and relieved, my friend drove three hours to pick up the prized gift but found when she arrived that they had just sold the last one and that the item had never been placed on hold for her in the first place. Talk about an irate customer! Imagine how you would feel if you had just driven three hours only to find out the product that you wanted has just been sold and is no longer available.

Customers expect products that they purchase to be safe, and they expect them to do what they advertise. Another woman purchased a knife sharpener endorsed by a celebrity chef that was so poorly constructed that it didn't even work one time. That woman will never purchase another product promoted by that chef and will probably not even watch that particular chef on TV ever again.

What Makes a Customer Difficult?

Knowing what the customer wants is only one part of the challenge in providing good customer service and dealing with difficult customers.

Customers can be difficult for a lot of different reasons, and you need to be able to adapt your response accordingly. Perhaps they're tired or stressed or frustrated. There may be things going on in their lives that have nothing to do with the product or service you provide, but the added emotional stress may make them much more sensitive when things don't go their way or they're not getting what they want. They may feel that no one's listening to them, so they feel they have to yell or make a scene just so they can be heard.

It could be that they were promised something that wasn't delivered. Or maybe they're just confused and don't understand your policies and procedures. Although it might surprise you, one of the best things that a difficult customer can do for you is to make a complaint. Customers complain for many reasons, but believe it or not, the main reason they complain is to give you an opportunity to fix the problem. Why else would a customer tell you about their negative experience? People complain because they feel they have been wronged or treated unfairly. All the same, they want to continue to do business with that establishment; otherwise, why wouldn't they just walk away and take their business elsewhere? If a customer gives you a chance to continue to do business together, you should make use of it.

Furthermore, the odds are that if one customer has had a problem, other customers may have experienced something similar. This allows you to fix any area where your business may not be meeting customer wants or expectations. Don't let your customer go running off to the competition; view all complaints as beneficial to you and your organization.

Types of Difficult Customers

Let's look at a few of the most common types of difficult customers and give you some tips on how to respond to them effectively.

First, let's talk about angry customers. Dealing with angry people requires a certain amount of caution. If you are to be effective in serving an angry customer, you need to move beyond the emotions to find out the reason for their anger. Here are some possible tactics.

First, be positive and stay positive. Make sure to tell the customer what you can do rather than what you *can't* do. If you say, "Our policy doesn't allow us to issue a refund," you can expect an angry response. But if you say, "I can offer you a credit that is valid at any of our stores," that's a positive answer, and it's much more likely to be accepted.

Acknowledge the customer's feelings of anger. Don't deny them by saying something like, "Oh, there's nothing to be mad about here," or "You really don't have to be upset." That can lead to major confrontation.

Instead, try to say something like, "I can see that you're upset. I want to help solve the problem, so please let me understand exactly what's happened." By taking this approach, you have acknowledged the customer's feelings, you've demonstrated a willingness to help, and you've asked them to participate in the problem-solving process.

Dissatisfied Customers

Let's now talk about dissatisfied customers. Sometimes a customer is dissatisfied with your product or service when you meet them in the first place. They may have been improperly served by you or by one of your peers, or even by a competitor, in the past. Even if you or your company was not involved in the previous experience, you represent your organization, and you may be considered just like that other person.

Even if the customer's suspicion or dissatisfaction has nothing to do with you, try to make them happy. Listen, and listen carefully. Often when people are upset, all they want to know is that you are willing to attend to their concerns. Again, remain positive. Even though the customer can drain your energy, don't get drawn into mirroring their anger or agreeing with their putdowns of your company, your products, or your services—or even your competitors.

><><><><><><><><><><><><><><><><><><><><><><><><><><><><><><><><><><><><><><><>

Often when people are upset, all they want to know is that you are willing to attend to their concerns.

><><><><><><><><><><><><><><><><><><><><><><><><><><><><><><><><><><><><><><><>

If appropriate, you should smile and interject positive comments into the conversation as you listen and try to determine an effective course of action. When you're dealing with difficult customers, always use positive wording. Instead of using the word *problem*, you should use words such as *situation* or *issue* or *concern* or maybe *challenge*. These are more positive words. Instead of saying *no* or *cannot*, you can say, "Well, what we *can* do is . . ." indicating that you want to correct the mistake. Instead of saying, "It's not my job" or "It's not my fault," you can say, "Although I don't ordinarily handle that, I'd be glad to assist you." Instead of saying, "You have to or you must . . ." you can say, "Would you mind. . . ?" or "Can I ask you to. . . ?" Don't say, "Our policy is . . ." Say, "While I'm unable to do plan A, what I can do is plan B." Make it positive.

Don't make excuses. Customers are typically not interested in why they did not get the product or service they thought they paid for. They want the problem solved in their favor. Again, always look for ways to correct the mistake, not cover it up. If you get defensive, you become a part of the problem and not a part of the solution.

Let's now take a look at indecisive customers. You will encounter people who cannot or will not make a decision. They sometimes spend hours vacillating back and forth. In some cases, they truly don't know what they want or what they need, as when, for example, they're looking for a gift for a special occasion. Sometimes these customers are afraid that they're going to choose incorrectly, so they get petrified by the indecision.

In these situations, you need to use all of your communication skills. It's important to be patient with the indecisive customer. Although they can be frustrating, they are still customers. You should ask open-ended questions just as you would do with a dissatisfied customer. Try to get them to share with you as much background information as possible to help you evaluate the situation and help them come to a decision; then you can suggest options.

Offer alternatives that will help in the decision-making process and reduce the customer's anxiety. Note that you are helping them; you are not making the decision for them. If you push your preferences off on them, they can blame you. Then they will very likely turn into dissatisfied customers, and you will have to deal with another difficult customer situation.

Next is demanding or domineering customers. Customers can be demanding or domineering for a number of reasons. Many times, domineering behavior is a part of a personality style. In other instances, it could be a reaction to a past customer experience or service encounter. A demanding customer may feel a need to be in or stay in control, especially if they felt out of control in the past.

Many times, domineering behavior is a part of a personality style.

With demanding customers, you should always be professional. Don't raise your voice or retaliate verbally. Don't let your behavior regress to childish name-calling, even if your customer is behaving that way. Show respect for your customer. This doesn't mean accommodating their every wish. It means that you should maintain positive eye contact, remain calm, use the customer's name, apologize if it's appropriate, and let the customer know that he or she is important to you and your company.

Next, we'll talk about rude or inconsiderate customers. Some people just seem to go out of their way to be offensive or get attention. Although they seem to be confident and self-assured outwardly, often they're insecure and defensive. They might raise their voices, demanding to speak to the supervisor, or they might be verbally abrupt, use profanity, ignore what you say, or otherwise go out of their way to be offensive.

With rude or inconsiderate customers, you should, again, remain professional. Just because the customer is exhibiting bad behavior doesn't justify your reacting in the same way. Remain calm, assertive, and in control. Don't resort to retaliation. Continue to show respect. Retaliation will only infuriate this type of customer, especially if they feel they've embarrassed themselves in the presence of others.

The last type of customer we'll talk about is the talkative type. Some customers spend an excessive amount of time discussing all types of things, such as personal experiences, family, friends, school accomplishments, other customer service situations, the weather—anything. You should remain warm and cordial, but try to stay focused. Recognize that this person is probably just naturally talkative. You can smile and acknowledge their comments and carry on brief conversations when you're helping them, but try to keep returning to the point. Respond to their questions politely so that you don't seem rude or abrupt, but then keep coming back with a business-related question, such as, "Is there anything else that I can help you with today?" It's up to you to manage the conversation. Keep in mind that you may be neglecting other customers by having to spend too much time with this one talkative person.

You might say something like, "I know you said you had a lot of shopping to do, so I won't keep you any longer. Thanks for coming in. I look forward to seeing you next time." Imply that you're ending this interaction to the benefit of the customer.

These are six of the most common types of difficult customers:

- Angry
- Dissatisfied
- Indecisive

- Demanding
- Rude
- Talkative

As we've seen, each type of difficult customer requires a different type of strategy. Learning to identify these key types will immediately help you respond to them in the most effective manner.

Now that we have a better understanding of what customers want and what makes them difficult, let's take a look at the seven steps that you can take to successfully resolve customer complaints and conflicts.

Seven Steps to Dealing with Difficult Customers

The key to employing these seven steps is taking them immediately. The moment that you learn that your customer is unhappy, don't let time lapse. You want to address the problem or issue directly. Avoidance will only make things worse.

1. Pay Attention

Listen intently. Stop doing what you're doing and pay careful attention to what the customer has to say. Don't interrupt, as this will only make the situation worse. Think about how you feel when someone interrupts you in the middle of a sentence. By talking about complaints, customers relieve some of the distress and ill feelings that they may have towards your establishment. The more the customer talks, the more you will learn about their concerns and issues. But be careful: often we don't listen, because as soon as a customer starts to complain, we may start to think about how we're going to respond to the situation or the accusations before we're done listening. Quite often, we already have a response, being ready to fight back.

Don't do that. Take a second and listen and relax. Listen to everything the customer has to say before you come up with your answer. On occasion complaining customers will be rude. They'll be angry, they'll use vulgar language, but stay the course and remain calm and level-headed. You might want to show that you're empathetic and understanding by saying things like, "I see and I can appreciate that; that must be upsetting." However, don't say these things unless you really mean them.

When the customer is done venting, repeat the problem in a calm, nonjudgmental tone. By repeating the problem, you've demonstrated your ability to the customer that you've heard and understood it. Basically, your customer wants to know that their concerns are being heard and that you are going to try to fix the problem.

> When the customer is done venting, repeat the problem in a calm, nonjudgmental tone.

If customers are ranting and not giving you a chance to explain or ask questions, use their names at the beginning or end of a sentence. People are more likely to listen when they hear their names. Ask open-ended questions to get to the root of the problem. Try to ask ones that prompt the customer to think about outcomes. For example, you might ask, "What could I do to try and make this situation better for you?" If the complaint is valid and the fault is yours, admit it. There's no weakness in admitting that something went wrong. The weakness occurs when something goes wrong and it's not addressed.

Don't be defensive. You'll get your chance to explain later. Again, no matter how great the temptation, do not take complaints personally. While you may feel that they're groundless, don't make an issue of it, because the customer feels the situation is important, and perception is reality. Make it clear that you want to help. Repeat the customer's concerns to make sure that you've understood the situation.

Be genuine and sincere in your response. Use a pleasant, concerned tone of voice, not a condescending or impatient tone. If there's been a mistake, apologize even if you personally are not to blame. Stay focused on your goal. The goal is achieving a mutually satisfactory resolution to the problem—a long-term, permanent fix. Concentrate your energy on coming up with an appropriate solution to the problem and use your best efforts in making the situation right.

Listen and clarify. Never defend or justify. A customer doesn't care if you are shorthanded or if you are having a bad day. They only care about being taken care of. No excuses, just solutions.

Ensure your customers understand that you believe them. This is the cornerstone of handling a complaint. Even if they may be lying or wrong about the situation, they still believe they have been wronged.

2. Thank the Customer

The second step is to thank the customer for bringing the problem to your attention. You can't resolve a problem if you're completely unaware of it or are making faulty assumptions about it. At the beginning, at the end, and in the middle—it doesn't matter when—thank the customer for complaining and making you aware of the situation.

Why would you do that? As we've already seen, with the simple act of complaining, your customer is telling you, "I care about your business and your success." They're giving you the opportunity to fix the problem and invite them back so that they can give you more money for your product or service. (That puts a different spin on the complaint, doesn't it?) Thank them for giving you a second chance, for letting you know that something in your establishment didn't work as it normally does, and for giving you a chance to make it right instead of allowing it to damage your reputation.

3. Apologize

The third step is apologizing. Sincerely convey to the customer your apology for the way the situation has made them feel. This is not a time for preachy reasons, justifications, or excuses; just apologize. Always apologize, even if you didn't do anything wrong. From your customer's perspective, they have a legitimate complaint, and they expect an apology. It could be as simple as, "I'm sorry we've inconvenienced you," or "I'm sorry. I know how frustrating it is to buy dinner and then not have everything when you get it home." A sincere apology will usually defuse a great deal of customer frustration.

But there is an exception to this rule. If a customer calls with a critical complaint, such as food poisoning, don't apologize, because it may be construed as an acceptance of guilt. Instead, refer to your company's policies on how to deal with any of those critical situations.

4. Seek the Best Solution

Determine what the customer wants as a solution. Ask them. They'll often surprise you by asking for less than you initially thought you would have to give, especially when they perceive your apology as genuinely sincere.

><><><><><><><><><><><><><><><><><><><><><><><><><><><><><><><><><><><><><><><

Determine what the customer wants as a solution. Ask them.

><><><><><><><><><><><><><><><><><><><><><><><><><><><><><><><><><><><><><><><

Then make it right. Ask the customer, "What can I do to make this right for you?" Be the judge of what is fair, of course, but allow them the opportunity to feel empowered in the situation. Many times, they may ask for the problem to be taken care of on their next visit, or they may want to know that you've talked to the person who made the mistake and you've corrected them. It's good to give customers the unexpected as well. Maybe a little freebie, an extra side, or a gift to show them that you care about them.

5. Reach an Agreement

Seek to agree on a solution that will resolve the situation to the customer's satisfaction. Your best intentions can miss the mark completely if you still fail to deliver what the customer wants. One particular four-letter word usually does the trick when seeking a solution to the customer's complaint, and that word is *fair.* "What do you think would be fair?" That word *fair* seems to bring out a sense of "All right, this is reasonable." Otherwise, customers may jump at the opportunity to demand inappropriate compensation for their trouble. Besides, the customer's main priority is resolving the issue.

Once that's done, extra benefits or compensation are just that—extra—although they can be important measures to take if you want customers to come back. If you ask the customer to propose a fair and reasonable solution, acting in partnership with you to find a resolution, chances are that it will consist of less than what you would have thought to have offered in the first place.

6. Take Action

Act on the solution with a sense of urgency. Customers will often respond more positively to your focus on helping them immediately versus than on the solution itself. Remember, one of the things that the customer wants is speed. Don't wait. Take action immediately.

7. Follow Up

Last but not least, follow up to ensure that the customer is completely satisfied, especially when you've had to enlist the help of others for the solution. Everything up to this point will be for nothing if the customer feels they are out of sight, out of mind.

We all know that problems happen. It's how you honestly acknowledge and handle them that counts with people. Customers will remember you and happily give you another chance to delight them when you choose to correct the problem with the best that you can offer, proving that you value them and their business.

Seven Steps to Dealing with Difficult Customers

1. Pay attention.
2. Thank the customer.
3. Apologize.
4. Seek the best solution.
5. Reach an agreement.
6. Take action.
7. Follow up.

Tips for Handling Difficult Customers

Now that we have walked through the seven steps in dealing with difficult customers, let's take a look at some additional tips that will help you stay focused and strong and enable you to easily move through the seven steps.

First and foremost, remember, do not take it personally. When a customer is difficult, they're unhappy with the product or the company. They are usually not unhappy with you, but even if they are, don't take it personally. Ultimately, it's not about you; it's about their needs not being met.

◇◇◇

Do not allow a customer to make you feel inadequate.

◇◇◇

Remember that you're good at what you do. Remind yourself of the skills that you have and why you're working there. Do not allow a customer to make you feel inadequate. Write down the complaints or concerns to show the customer that you're listening by recording the problem. Even if you're on the phone, tell the customer that you're writing down the details. This will also give you a written record of the issues for future reference. When the issue is documented, you now have a record of past complaints and concerns and can start to see patterns or trends that may need to be addressed.

If a customer is becoming more difficult, invite a supervisor to join the two of you. The customer will notice that you're treating them as important by seeking additional help. This also is a great way to get more support for yourself personally and learn additional ways that your supervisor deals with dissatisfied customers.

When the customer leaves, debrief the situation with someone else. Sometimes you may need to talk about your difficult customer to get rid of negative thoughts or emotions.

This is really important. You need to allow yourself to let go of any of the leftover negativity from the experience, so that it does not affect you personally or professionally. There's nothing worse than taking a bad experience home with you. Let go of all the negativity of the day before you leave work. You can do this by debriefing.

It is also good to learn some stress management techniques. Stress management techniques can help you stay calm if a customer raises their voice or becomes angry or emotional. By learning to breathe deeply and focus on the positives, you can ensure that your body doesn't carry around excess stress that can be detrimental to your health. Learning these techniques can help you to handle difficult customers with ease without getting upset yourself, and to recognize and accept the unavoidable fact that you will work with customers who are having a bad day. When people are having a bad day, anything and everything can upset them, even the smallest of glitches. Understand that when you're working with the public, some people will take their bad day out on you, so don't take it personally. Once the experience is over, consider what you could do differently next time.

If the customer is complaining about the company, a system, or a process, review it and determine if something needs to be changed. Think about the way that you handled the customer, and note anything that you would do differently next time. Learn from each experience, and hone your skills in working with people. It is invaluable and will help you in future situations and in any type of job that interacts directly with customers.

Finally, engage in ongoing learning. Invest in yourself and in your ongoing personal development. The stronger and more confident you are as a person, the easier it will be to handle stressful situations. You can attend local workshops and seminars, read books, or watch classes online. Practice with role playing and prepare yourself with common customer service scenarios.

◇◇◇

Engage in ongoing learning.

◇◇◇

These skills can help you in all aspects of life, personally and professionally. Most of us deal with many people on a day-to-day basis: customers, coworkers, friends, families, even strangers. When you feel good about yourself and you know how to work with people, you can easily handle any type of upset customer and bring more happiness and peace into your life as well as the lives of others.

When the Customer Isn't Right

We've all heard the saying, "The customer is always right." But we already know that the customer is *not* always right. What do you do then?

Does it really matter if you are the one that's right? You can win the fight, but you may lose a customer. Given a choice between acknowledging that a customer is upset and proving that he or she is wrong, which would you choose? You can be right, or you can have empathy. You can't have both.

You can be right, or you can have empathy. You can't have both.

Smart service providers understand that the word *right* in "The customer is always right" doesn't mean that they'd win in court or a debate. It means that if you want the customer to remain a customer, you need to permit them to believe that they're right. If someone thinks they're unhappy, then you know what? They're unhappy.

When you are in the customer service business, you will inevitably come across people who just seem to be jerks. For some reason, they may even relish being a jerk, and there's no satisfying them.

The customer is not always right, but the customer may be *feeling* right. That is their reality, and as customer service providers, we have to take the high road and figure out what is causing them to feel the way they do. Focus and recognize that they feel right and we have to respect their feelings. If we had any part in their upset, we are the ones that need to make it right. Even if we didn't, we should still make it right, because that's good customer service. Great service can go a long way in reducing the number of difficult customer experiences that you encounter and will need to deal with.

Great customer service goes beyond a smile and helpful information. It's an attitude about work and people. Good customer service is a philosophy. It is also about techniques and strategies that can be learned through education, training, and patience.

Preventing Difficult Customer Situations

Although there will always be difficult customers and difficult situations, there are some ways in which you can be proactive and prevent some difficult customer situations before they happen. You can utilize the information that we've already covered in this book to deal with situations when they arise, but don't wait for difficult situations. Prevent them from happening in the first place.

> Don't wait for difficult situations. Prevent them from happening in the first place.

To help you prevent difficult customer situations before they happen, let's look at some pitfalls to avoid. The first thing to keep in mind is to always use positive language. This also holds true for nonverbal language. Make sure that the signals that you're giving out give your customers a positive impression.

Nine Negative Signals

Here are nine negative signals to avoid when dealing with customers.

1. **Avoid giving wrong facial expressions.** Always be aware of your facial expressions when you're communicating with a customer, especially if they're upset about something. Check with your coworkers, supervisors, or friends, and ask them whether you're displaying any annoying facial expressions, like rolling your eyes, scowling, or smiling in an inappropriate way, when you're experiencing a tense or unhappy situation. It is best to provide a calm, sincere, concerned, and interested facial expression. Show the customer that you care, appreciate, and acknowledge their feedback as well as the complaint or unpleasant experience if that's the case.

Avoid smiling when a customer is expressing anger.

If you do, you may upset the customer even more by making them feel that you're not taking their issue seriously.

2. **Avoid using an annoying voice tone.** Did you know that people respond more to *how* you say something than to *what* you say? When you sound annoyed, impatient, or condescending, you are going to make an upset customer even angrier. Conversely, when you sound confident, the customer will believe that you know what you're talking about. Eventually it will be much easier for you to calm them down.

You sound annoyed when your tone goes up at the end of the sentence; it will make you sound as if you're asking a question. Record and listen to yourself talking. If you hear your tone going up at the end of the sentence, practice ending your sentences on a lower note.

When you're talking to upset customers, you will calm them down much easier and faster when you respond to them in a calm, firm, caring, and soothing tone.

3. **Avoid closed, defensive, crossed-armed gestures.** These indicate defensiveness, unwillingness to listen, and a resolutely closed mind. When you are attending to an upset or angry customer, uncross your arms to display your openness and show that you're listening attentively.

4. **Avoid negative body postures.** Always maintain an open, nonthreatening body posture to avoid increasing the irritation of a difficult customer. Don't crowd them; provide enough personal space by standing far enough away. Stand or sit up straight to show that you're being attentive and listening. Avoid slumping or slouching, as you'll be seen as inattentive or uninterested.

5. **Avoid touching and physical contact.** Avoid touching a difficult or upset person at all times, as it may provoke them further and may lead towards violence.

6. **Avoid cursing and swearing.** Remain calm and respond with patience when someone is cursing and swearing at you. This is a sign of strength, not of weakness. Always compose yourself in a calm and steady manner when responding to an angry or difficult customer. Remember that you are a professional representing your company. There's never an excuse for you to curse or swear, even if the customer does so.

7. Avoid eating, chewing, and nibbling when you are communicating with a customer, either through the phone or face-to-face. Don't chew gum, eat, or nibble on any food. Customers consider these very annoying, and they will further upset someone who is already irate.

8. Avoid sighing. Don't sigh in front of an angry or upset customer. It only suggests annoyance, impatience, and dissatisfaction and will worsen an already tense situation.

9. Avoid slow movement. Angry and upset customers are already in an impatient mood, and they expect you to respond to their needs and requests with speed. Move swiftly, and don't dawdle when you're assisting a difficult customer.

Nine Signals to Avoid

1. Wrong facial expressions
2. An annoying voice tone
3. Closed, defensive gestures
4. Negative body postures
5. Touching and physical contact
6. Cursing or swearing
7. Eating, chewing, or nibbling
8. Sighing
9. Slow movement

Preventing Complaints

Here are five tips to prevent some complaints before they happen:

1. **Follow the standards of your organization.** Review your employee handbook or other relevant material for advice on how your company handles customer service situations. You need to be in line with your company's position on customer service. You'll have trouble doing that if you're not familiar with its policies.

2. **Work on controlling your inflection and tone of voice.** You can practice giving calm responses when you're alone, or you can have role-playing sessions with your coworkers. Maintaining a polite, positive tone of voice is key to good customer service.

3. **Listen to your customer.** Try to understand what they're requesting and attempt to understand any under-lying concerns that are not being expressed. If you can understand your customer's needs, you can better help meet their needs.

4. **Always be positive, friendly, and helpful, and have a good attitude.** If a customer is having a difficult experience or is being difficult, control the situation by remaining calm and in control. Engage with a difficult customer as a human being and be sure to thank them for their business.

5. **Be receptive to feedback.** If you receive either praise or a complaint, give it consideration, and use it to work towards your future customer service goals.

Tips for Preventing Complaints

1. Follow your organization's standards.
2. Control your inflection and tone of voice.
3. Listen to your customer.
4. Always be positive.
5. Be receptive to feedback.

Using Body Language

Now let's talk about using body language to improve your customer service. The way you stand and look at a customer can speak more than your words. Maintain eye contact. As previously noted, don't cross your arms over your chest. Avoid closed, unapproachable postures and gestures. If you're feeling defensive, avoid the urge to roll your eyes. If you're feeling exasperated, nod and smile, no matter how irritated you may feel. This shows that you value your customer's opinion and your customer's business.

Use body language to quickly improve your customer service skills. People use many different methods for getting an idea across. It's not just the words you say: there are other factors to take into account. Your body language is the foundation of all communication. Body language conveys the majority of what we say. Take extra care to use proper body language with customers if you want them to feel satisfied with your service.

Here are five simple things that you can do to improve your body language and your customer service skills:

1. **Keep eye contact.** The easiest way to ensure that the customer knows that you're paying attention to them and care about what they say is to keep eye contact with them as much as possible. Eye contact says, "You are the only person that I'm listening to right now." It's the most overlooked aspect of body language, and it's easy to forget when you're trying to handle multiple things at once.

When you're dealing with a difficult customer, try to make eye contact with them as you are speaking. While they are speaking, don't stare at them, or they might feel awkward; just try to keep a delicate balance between eye contact and no eye contact. Be friendly, but don't be strange.

2. **Face your customer.** Actors have an important body language tool from which the service industry could really benefit. Actors know that they should face the front of their body to the camera or the audience as much as possible without looking unnatural.

You can use this tool when you're speaking to your customers, especially difficult ones. Make sure to face them with the front of your body as much as you can. You don't want to turn your back on them, and you don't want to stay turned in profile, because that will tell them that you're not interested in what they have to say. We're always interested in what the customer has to say, so make sure they know that.

3. **Always direct with an open hand.** This is one of the subtler techniques. Whenever you're giving directions to someone, use an open hand gesture. If you point with your index finger or your thumb, as we often do in everyday life, it can come across as rude. Open hands are inviting, and pointed fingers are dismissive. Your body language will be saying, "Allow me to show you the right way," or "Allow me to show you this way with an open hand."

4. **Maintain good posture.** Posture is one of the most important aspects of body language. Posture is like a shortcut to knowing a person's mood. The best posture is simply a military at-ease position. Keep your spine straight, your legs a bit apart, and your hands behind your back. This will push your chest out, and hopefully it'll keep your chin raised. You never want to slouch or lower your chin, as this gives an impression that you're in a bad mood or that you're lazy and you don't feel like helping anyone.

5. **Make sure to smile.** I know what you're saying: "Of course we smile; that's the first thing that we do." Smiling lets customers know that you're paying attention to them. It gives them the impression that you truly care and enjoy what you're doing. Be careful to smile properly, because some smiles can look forced and disingenuous, and that's the opposite of what you want. Smile with your eyes as much as your mouth.

A good smile goes a long way in ensuring satisfaction. Your body language, signals, and gestures will constantly project your attitude in the public eye. Always make sure that your attitude is, "I'll go the extra mile to help you, and I'll assist you the best I can." Keep in mind that you will expect the same quality of service when you are the customer.

Tips for Improving Your Body Language

1. Keep eye contact.
2. Face your customer.
3. Direct with an open hand.
4. Maintain good posture.
5. Make sure to smile.

Key Points in This Chapter

1. Understand customers and what they want and expect.
2. Understand what makes a customer difficult.
3. Learn Seven steps to dealing with difficult customers.
4. Learn Additional tips for handling difficult customers.
5. Prevent difficult customer situations before they happen.

THREE

Effective Online Customer Support

n this chapter, we'll go over techniques that will enhance your customer support chat conversations. We'll talk about how chat is different from other kinds of conversations and how to hone your replies for the chat audience. We'll also talk through a typical chat sequence and learn about the mistakes to avoid.

First, we'll walk through why live chat is so popular with customers and explore how it's different from other support venues. This will be followed by identifying the best practices used by successful agents to ensure a successful support session.

Then we'll focus on how to avoid common mistakes and how to manage negativity bias. Finally, we'll look at specific business writing styles you can tailor to a chat customer experience.

Why Live Chat Support?

To better understand the importance of this topic, let's look at why businesses—both business-to-business and business-to-consumer—are increasingly turning to live chat for customer support. Even as far back as 2010, 44 percent of online consumers said that having questions answered by a live person while they were in the middle of an online purchase was one of the most important features a website can offer. (This was according to Forrester Research and Guidance Services.) Moreover, 38 percent of the customers who used chat while they were shopping were influenced by that conversation in deciding to make the purchase. Kayako, which is a help desk technology company, regularly reviews their customer's interactions. They say that 52 percent of consumers are more loyal to companies that offer live chat support.

Live chat provides important insights. With live chat, the business has access to customers' chat histories, which can be sorted, searched, and filtered. The business can learn more about the problems their customers are frequently running into. It can also teach you what questions are being asked during a sales cycle.

Live chat offers faster resolutions with lower investment of employee time. Chats allow agents to address multiple clients simultaneously as well as offering real-time conversation, with the ability to share links, collect information, and save a full transcript for later reference. According to the American Customer Satisfaction Index, a cross-industry measure of customer satisfaction nationwide, live chat has received 88 percent average satisfaction rating as a customer service channel.

Live chat offers faster resolutions with lower investment of employee time.

Let's dig into that last figure a little bit more. Seventy-three percent of customers say live chat is the most comfortable way to communicate with a business compared to email, at 61 percent, or traditional phone support, at 44 percent. Customers report liking the fact that they can multitask while they're resolving an issue. They're also more comfortable initiating support chats at work, where phone conversations could be overheard or distract their colleagues. Chat also offers the benefits of conversation without being completely tied down during that conversation. Many people are more comfortable writing in short back-and-forth chats than in an email, which comes off as more formal and is a long form style.

Chat is also fast—or should be. A customer who receives excellent response to their email inquiry in an hour or two may be satisfied, but the customer who receives the exact same answer in real time via live chat will often be even happier, because they can continue on with their task immediately. This could be extremely important if the customer makes a purchase decision: they'll continue to move through the sale without losing momentum or choosing another option.

This touches on another benefit: online chat offers help where and when the customer is already working. Whether they're already shopping online or researching a problem, online chat lets them get their answers without switching communication tools or having to look up a phone number or dig up an email address.

In short, businesses like live chat, and customers like it. In fact, customer preference is driving the increase in adoption of online customer service.

> ◇◇
>
> ## Customer preference is driving the increase in adoption of online customer service.
>
> ◇◇

As a result, keeping in mind what a customer wants from the experience will be key to approaching the techniques we'll talk about. Ninety-five percent of customers say they'd prefer slower support if it meant the quality of help was higher. Even though 24 percent of customers say that long wait times are their biggest frustration, they are also more satisfied by slower and more personalized expert support than by fast but low-quality support. Comm100, another customer service technology company, analyzed their client interactions and learned that companies with satisfaction ratings above 90 percent have longer chat durations, at an average of 11 minutes and 47 seconds. That's more than three minutes longer than those with below 90 percent ratings.

They also saw that organizations with higher wait times tended to have higher customer satisfaction ratings than those with lower wait times. This means that it's not necessarily better to optimize for speed if it means compromising on quality. Zendesk, a customer service software firm, found that 49 percent of their clients' customers expect agents they're chatting with to be empathetic and to sound human in their responses. This will impact your writing style, your approach to offering solutions, and how and when you use scripted responses. And 73 percent of customers say that valuing their time is the most important thing companies can do to provide good customer service.

What Makes Live Chat Different?

Now let's look at exactly what makes chat support different from other forms of support communication. As something between verbal conversation and email, text chat is both and neither at the same time. One big difference between chat and email support is that chat is synchronous, meaning both parties are engaged at the same time in the same digital place. While an email conversation takes place over hours or even days, customers expect chat agents to be present in a prompt back-and-forth exchange. This requires conversational writing but allows information to be shared organically in small chunks instead of having to dump as much as possible into one giant message, as you would with an email answer.

People are also more likely to use chat when they want an answer to a question while they're in the middle of a task. Chat is synchronous not only with the agent but also with the customer's workflow. They want to resolve their problem or at least see the next step toward that resolution during the session so they can get back to completing their task.

Unlike phone support, chat is a text-based medium, meaning that neither party will have verbal or visual context clues that help during communication. This often leads to what is called *negativity bias* in written discussions.

Another way to describe chat support is to compare it to text messaging, which we all do with friends and family on our phones.

Some of this familiarity does impact customer expectations. Chat texts, like their smartphone counterparts, are typically short and simple. You'll write in concise, jargon-free snippets and greet the customer personally by name. The best agents are even able to use expressions and interjections such as *woo!* and *oops!* or even a carefully chosen emoji at just the right moment to create an experience that feels human and personal while remaining professional and respectful—which is of course how chat support differs from text messaging with friends.

Personal texting also allows for a much greater range of shorthand, such as IMHO and BRB and creative spellings that aren't appropriate in a customer support setting, where all communication must be accurate in grammar, spelling, and information shared. A friend might text the letter K as a response, but that will be perceived as flippant or hasty by a customer. Integrating text-based conversation with an informal yet professional tone might be the trickiest part of online support. We will talk more in depth about all these details later in this chapter.

Key Factors for Successful Online Chat

Live, in-person communication is information-rich. You will use facial expressions, voice inflections, body language, and the pace of response to get context during even a simple conversation. Our brains are very good at taking all these clues in to determine if the person you're talking to is happy or sad, sarcastic or annoyed, angry or just focused.

It's not hard, then, to imagine that a chat conversation that uses only verbal inputs puts both sides at a disadvantage. Without the usual set of social clues, we tend to interpret written messages as more negative. Positive statements become neutral; neutral statements become negative. This is called *negativity bias*.

⬦⬦

Without the usual social clues, we tend to interpret written messages as more negative. This is called *negativity bias*.

⬦⬦

A *New York Times* columnist described a scenario when he was working with his publisher on details for a book contract via email. He thought the conversation was going well until his publisher wrote, "It's difficult to have this conversation by email. I sound strident, and you sound exasperated." The writer had no idea he was coming off as exasperated, which was causing the publisher to respond with negative emotions.

Since emotion drives the biggest impact in customer satisfaction, managing positivity is critical. We will go in depth on this subject later in this chapter, during our next section on managing customer experience, where we will discuss techniques that can counter negativity bias.

Staying in control of the session is key to a positive experience for both you and the customer. Neither of you has access to the verbal and visual clues used to know that the other person is about to speak. Messages can pile up or overlap, causing confusion and possibly misunderstanding. It's up to you to pace the conversation so that messages remain sequential. Build firm boundaries as you lead, and don't be afraid to ask customers to focus on one thing at a time rather than letting them continue an endless stream of thoughts and details.

Tell the customer what you need and send specific directions on what they have to do to help you resolve the session. Then communicate each step as you go, so that the customer knows what to expect. Surprised people tend to behave badly. If you need time to find an answer or research a problem, tell the customer that will happen so they don't panic when you're silent for a few minutes. Tell them the things they will have to do, so they aren't surprised if you have to ask them to click on something or perform a task. And of course, tell them up front about any limitations you anticipate so they're not surprised that you can't magically reboot their phone from a desktop or give you a 100 percent discount.

Unlike with an email support answer, with chat, you don't have to dump everything into one long reply. Instead, introduce ideas or actions one at a time. Then let the customer respond to make sure they've understood and are still on the same page as you.

If the customer has asked several questions, answer them one at a time. If questions are complex, break them down into bite-size, easily answered chunks. Do the same with long or complicated answers. Break them down so that each message is a single, understandable element of the longer answer. Support statistics usually speak in terms of speed and timing of responses, but when striving for a high-quality support experience, think in terms of efficiency instead. Typing quickly means that you are using most of your time to create the responses instead of just typing that response in.

Many of your efficiencies are going to come from a skilled use of available tools. Text expanders and saved replies, for example, can often turn long phrases that are typed into two or three keystrokes. Much like learning keyboard shortcuts on software, these tools can be more efficient than clicking several open menus. You might spend a little extra time setting them up and learning to use them, but that time will be repaid many times over in efficiency.

If you have the ability to access a knowledge base, make sure to use it for looking up steps that you copy and paste instead of rewriting over and over, or, even better, turning the steps over to the customer themselves so that they can use them at their own pace.

Customers dislike impersonal interactions, which make them feel as if they're talking to a chat bot instead of a real person. On the other hand, there are many phrases and interactions that agents will repeat over and over and over every day. The key is balancing personalization with efficiency.

∞

Customers dislike impersonal interactions.

∞

Greetings and closing statements are likely to be very similar with each call, so they become good candidates. The key to high-quality support is to personalize even these common interactions where possible. A typical greeting might be, "Thank you for contacting us." Even better would be, "Thank you for contacting us with your questions about ABC product." Personalize your message to what the customer's asking about.

Other areas where scripts and hot keys work well are with requests for common information, such as hours of operation, dates of events, phone numbers, and the like. Your organization may also offer people the ability to submit feature requests or refund requests. When you're collecting information that is essentially a chat version of a web form, scripts and hot keys will save you lots of effort. You can also research conversations, find phrases that are used over and over, and save those for reuse. This can be especially helpful when the conversation is tense and you want to have calming or deescalating phrases ready to go when you yourself might be feeling tense. Just make sure that all responses are crafted so that they encourage customization in the moment. A perfect canned response shouldn't sound canned at all.

A perfect canned response shouldn't sound canned at all.

Empathy in a Support Setting

Empathy in a support setting is somewhat different than we might think of it in everyday life, but we can use some of the same language. In a business context, empathy is understanding your client's point of view and reflecting that in your actions and responses. This is different from problem-solving.

A solution that doesn't take into account your customer's point of view is going to feel wrong to the customer even if it solves the problem technically. Suggesting an expensive upgrade is not going to result in satisfaction for a cost-sensitive customer, and the converse can be true: complicated workarounds to save a few dollars won't sit right with a customer who just needs a feature to be easy and convenient. Empathy, then, is about offering solutions that fit or offering choices so the customer can tell you where their priorities lie.

Even better, hone your conversation to learn the customer's priorities as you go. Much of this communication is a bit harder in a chat setting, so here are a few things to keep at the front of your mind with chats that you might not have to think about when speaking.

When we text friends and family, we don't usually use their names or include salutations. We know whom we're talking to, and the conversation is ongoing. In a support setting, though, remember to include names when appropriate, and work to craft messages that are pleasant, including greetings, introductions, even transitions.

Small talk is also much easier in verbal conversation. It will take some practice to work in written small talk without sounding forced or insincere. Review conversations at your organization to see what other agents have done and whether you think the interactions worked and why.

Like the best party icebreakers, a simple quick line like, "Oh, you're in Texas; I hear it's really hot there right now," can relax a customer and make them more comfortable during the conversation. Taking the time to listen and have a natural conversation with your customer may even require you to anticipate a need before they spot it themselves; in that case, you will become the hero of the moment. This can take the form of spotting a potential conflict or pointing out how another solution could be even better than the one they are asking for. You can also prepare links to documentation or training material and show that you're looking beyond the session for ways to continue to be helpful.

Every chat conversation is detective work that is trying, in as few exchanges as possible, to understand a problem or a situation based solely on what another person is typing.

The faster you can puzzle out the actual problem, the happier your client will be. If the customer keeps typing more and more questions, you may have to take control of the conversation and start teasing out the real meaning behind them. Your willingness to understand your customer's true issue is part of the definition of empathy.

Managing Customer Experience

In this section then we'll talk about how to overcome some of the common problems and customer pet peeves that are unique to a chat support setting. Keeping negativity bias at the top of your mind will be very important in all chat communication, but it's not impossible to overcome; you'll just have to get your words to work a little harder for you. Start by looking for stop words and form a habit of restructuring them with a positive angle. Words and phrases that you should stop using include those that imply a barrier that the customer feels they can't overcome. Words like *can't, won't,* and pretty much any other *not* contractions fall into this category.

Expressions like *unfortunately* or *I'm sorry* are reserved for actual apologies. They're not to be used when you simply mean you need to look something up or ask another question.

Using expressions like these is often a holdover from verbal communication, where you might say, "Oh, sorry; can I ask you more about X, Y, Z?" But when written, that *sorry* becomes a stumbling block the customers may not get past or, in the worst case, might hear as sarcastic.

Additionally, your employer or your organization may provide you with terms that have negative connotations in your specific industry. One style guide preferred the use of the phrase *system disruption* instead of *outage* when referring to their service being offline. Another software style guide suggests *surprising* or *abnormal result* instead of *glitch* or *bug*. Many companies like to use *our preferred method* or something similar instead of *policy*, as the word *policy* often carries negative connotations of strictness and inflexibility. Check your style guide and watch for those additional stop words.

Avoiding negative words can then help you reframe bad-news statements into good-news statements. Instead of "Our technician isn't available right now; they'll look at it tomorrow" (see the *not* word in there?), reframe: "Our technician will address your issue first thing when they return to work tomorrow morning." This transitions the bad news—*not available*—into good news: my problem will be solved tomorrow. Instead of stopping progress by stating what you can't do, state what you can do, such as directing the customer to a guide that will solve the problem.

As a quick aside, the word *because* is a powerful psychological device. People are more likely to comply with a request or accept a condition when a *because* is given, even if the "because" reason isn't that compelling; it's the word itself that creates the response.

◇◇◇

People are more likely to comply with a request or accept a condition when a *because* is given.

◇◇◇

Short and simple is best, but this must be held in the context of keeping negativity at bay. Sometimes taking a little longer is better for managing positivity. You might have noticed that the good-news statements above are longer than the shorter, negative statements. This is because without those extra bodily and verbal clues, texts sometimes must work harder to include context, avoid negative words, or convey empathy.

Perhaps to paint this picture, we can look at a couple of extreme examples. Imagine you're conversing in a text thread with a friend and you've just spent five minutes describing a problem in your life. How would you feel if they responded with a bald "OK"? In this context, "OK" is short, but feels dismissive and inattentive. In a support setting, it will sound frustrating. Here's an alternative: "Let's make that task easier, using some shortcuts I can show you." This will go a long way further towards redirecting the bad feelings in the complaint than just "OK."

Here's another one. As you are wrapping up, how do you think a customer would respond to the message, "Anything else?" It's likely that they would hear this as, "Anything else?

I really need to move on." Instead, try the slightly longer expression, "Is there anything else I can help you with?"

These are techniques you probably already use to some degree, if not all the time. But they become extremely important in a chat context, where someone may already be in a negative mindset and may be even more likely to fall into negativity bias.

Chat and Text Etiquette

Chat and text communication has its own set of etiquette, which can differ from everyday language or email communication. It has to do with punctuation and emoticons. Help Scout, a customer support solutions company coaches agents to use exclamation points and emoticons in written support responses. They have seen agents' overall customer ratings improve just from this one technique. They also say that subject matter experts who use emoticons are perceived as more friendly and competent than those who don't. Compare these two replies, read them, and think about the tone you hear in your head as you do:

"Hey, David, I see what you're saying. I've fixed the data on that sheet. If you see this again, send a list of the files that need updating."

Now here's the second one: "Hey David! I see what you're saying! I've fixed the data on that sheet. If you see this again, send a list of the files that need updating." ☺

It's the same exact message, but the exclamations after the salutation and the expression of understanding subtly change the tone from annoyed to enthusiastic. The smiley face changes the tone from demanding to cooperative.

Emojis can convey anything from neutral happiness to sarcastic annoyance. Gone are the days when emoticons were universally considered unprofessional. Business communication tools like Slack have comfortably expanded their use into the workplace, and a generation of texters has grown up using them to convey tone that is part of missing context clues.

Gone are the days when emoticons were considered unprofessional.

Consider *OK*, the example from earlier. By itself, *OK* is not only neutral, it is so neutral that it can be interpreted many different ways, most likely negative. Consider then how simply adding an emoji can clarify the intent of the sender.

A sad face can say, "I'm sorry to hear that." An exploding brain emoji can say, "I can't believe he'd do that," and a broken heart emoji can convey empathy for the sender. This example is not to say that *OK* plus an emoji is the correct response, but to illustrate how an emoji can drastically change text interpretation.

This leads us to the first rule of thumb for including emoticons and emojis in a professional support setting: use them when they add emotional clarity to your response. A well-placed frowny face after the phrase, "That sounds so frustrating," can amp up the perception of empathy, just as a smiley face after, "Let's figure this out," can reassure the reader that you are not annoyed. Using them outside of this context, however, can cross the line into seeming unprofessional or just silly.

Another point: if your customer greets you with a smiley face right off the bat or a very informal, "Hi there," responding in kind can show that you are on their wavelength. The opposite is true, of course. If the customer's writing or title or question is terse or formal, then avoid emojis until you get a read on their personality.

Even if you work emojis into your style, stick with the basic face icons. Beyond these very familiar symbols, you get into varying interpretations that could cause problems. For example, one heavily used iPhone emoji can mean clapping to some people and praying to others.

Here is a generational difference that can cause confusion. Gen Z people often construe messages that end with a period to indicate annoyance. Putting a period at the end of a casually texted thought could mean you're raring for a fight. The premise is that periods have become unnecessary because of the technology itself. It's obvious your thought has ended: it's displayed in a bubble, separate from other thoughts, to an audience comfortable with very casual texting, minimal punctuation, and lots of shorthand. A complete sentence with punctuation can feel very formal, which, without other context clues, can be interpreted as if you are speaking through gritted teeth right before you explode. It can also seem to younger recipients that the sender isn't comfortable with them or is being overly polite in a suspicious or judgmental way. As we've seen, chat support is not texting, but it's important to be aware of this convention, especially if you frequently support younger generations at your organization. Step two is to apply the convention deliberately.

Here are two simple rules. If your company style guide allows, you can easily avoid periods at the end of submitted messages. On the other hand, periods that break up sentences in the same message bubble are fine.

Never use a period for a one-word reply in a chat.

Second, never use a period for a one-word reply: *OK*, *yes*, *sure*, and the dreaded *fine*. Also consider leaving them off for short phrases such as *got it* or *let me see* kinds of phrases. Even in the context of a longer reply, a period after *OK*, *yes*, and *sure* can be perceived as snippy, so avoid the period and consider using an exclamation point or no punctuation at all.

Speaking of exclamation points, here's a quick rule of thumb for them: just like with emojis, use them when you need to make sure you are communicating positivity when that might be unclear, although using too many can come across as insincere, overexcited, or thoughtless. You don't need an exclamation point in every sentence: just on the ones that might be heard more negatively.

Here are three other punctuation guidelines to consider. Ellipses—those three-dot symbols of a trailed-off thought—create a sense of uncertainty. Definitely don't use them as a substitute for a period at the end of sentences, which will create confusion or could be heard as sarcastic. Used to break up a thought, ellipses can create anticipation or tension. It might be tempting to use an ellipse after *this will only take two or three minutes to complete, I'll get back to you shortly*. But the result might be anxiety instead of reassurance. Imagine an ellipse as a shrug with a question mark: *I'll get back to you shortly* . . .

Avoid dashes as punctuation between phrases. Dashes (of different lengths) are still used in compound words or when you're writing a range of times and dates, but if you find yourself using them to construct complex sentences, it's probably time to simplify your thought.

Apart from these chat-specific quirks, you'll otherwise use commas and question marks and periods between sentences in the same bubble as usual.

Customers' Pet Peeves

At this point, let's stop to identify the biggest customer pet peeves. Like with negativity bias, you won't be able to avoid all of these situations, but being aware of them can help you mitigate and talk the customer through them as positively as possible. These are not in any specific order, just the ones that are the most common. This list covers issues over which you may or may not have control, but they're included so that when you do have control, you can fix them; when you don't, you can prepare responses to mitigate them.

Technical issues are certainly out of an agent's control, especially if they're on the client side. Poor Internet connections, broken equipment, or power outages can frustrate even the most skilled team. Prepare for the issues you can manage and have workarounds in your back pocket. If someone's having Internet issues on their computer, ask them to log in on their phone, or vice versa.

Your organization may dictate the customer experience before they ever get close to an agent. Just be aware that a common pet peeve is having to fill out forms calling for lots of information that feels irrelevant before the customer is even asked about their problem. If possible, recommend to management that some questions be saved for later or removed if they're there only for marketing. When you are opening a session and have to ask your questions, make sure you stick to those that are working on the problem. While customers are willing to wait a bit for high-quality support, long waits are frustrating and create a negative mood overall.

>>

A common pet peeve is having to fill out forms calling for lots of information.

>>

If you're feeling overwhelmed or stretched to the point of slowing down, be aware of your personal limits and change your availability settings. If your organization works along topic lines, you may have to transfer customers to the correct specialist. In these cases, you can't control the workflow, but you can use your positivity techniques to make the experience as easy as possible. Part of that ease is making sure that the new agent has all the information they will need so that they can simply jump in and continue instead of asking customers to repeat themselves (which is another pet peeve). Do what you can to prevent stacking them up.

You'll have to find a balance between professional and friendly: impersonal responses are a major pet peeve. Making incorrect assumptions about the client—such as their age, gender, or the knowledge they have—is a faux pas in any support setting, When you have even fewer clues as to a person's identity, this could be far trickier. One woman who has a very unusual name that's not easily gendered recently had a negative experience with a sales chat agent who assumed that because she was inquiring about accounting software, she was male. She mentioned her spouse and business partner. The agent then referred to that partner as "your wife," to which she had to reply, "I *am* the wife." Notice that simply using the client's own language—"spouse and business partner"—would have worked just as well and avoided the problem.

Lack of knowledge refers to knowledge about the specific question being asked. Sometimes a customer will end up in the wrong chat. Rather than try to wing it, direct them to the person who can help. Customers don't like to be transferred (another major pet peeve), but they will catch on quickly if you aren't familiar with their issue or have to research answers over and over.

Our last pet peeve is unique to chat. Conventions for ending a phone call are well-known, but they are far less established for chat. You may feel that you've answered all the customer's questions and be reasonably sure the conversation is over, yet still get a negative review for ending abruptly if you don't close the session clearly and positively.

Constructing Conversation Flow

As the cliché has it, you never get a second chance to make a first impression. This can be especially true in the context of chat support, where half the people are reaching out with skepticism and the other half with unrealistic expectations about how much you can figure out telepathically through a screen.

Setting a personable professional tone from the start can make the entire session go more smoothly. Begin by accepting the connection as quickly as possible. Remember that in chat, customers are most likely to be in the middle of a task that has been delayed by the question they need to answer. Especially for that first set of interactions, give them your full attention. Even if you manage multiple sessions, reserve focus time as much as possible for those first critical interactions. Once reassured, chatters will be more comfortable with a slower pace later in the session.

As you prepare to accept a chat session and/or while you're completing the initial greetings, learn everything you can about the question and the customer. If your system allows them to submit the question before the chat is initiated, make sure to read it very carefully. Before you start to interact, have a sense of what questions you need to ask and what the solution might be, so you can include this information in your personalization right from the start.

Similarly, if you are working with known accounts and registered users, call up the account and have it at hand from the beginning. Customers hate repeating themselves, but they often assume that since they are customers, you should know everything about them. To them, repeating may mean they have to give you information they think you should have.

Customers hate repeating themselves.

As you craft your greetings for these first moments—whether they are prewritten or on the fly—hitting the balance between professional and friendly is critical. Take the time to include *hi!, hello!,* or *welcome back!* as appropriate. Include the customer's name, if provided, and ask for it if not. This will show that you see them as an individual, not just as a ticket. Provide Support, a customer support provider and consulting company, even recommends saying, "Hello, John, how are you doing?" reporting that customers are often positively surprised by the question. Create an opening for familiarity and for the customer to share their problem in an organic way.

You can also briefly introduce yourself, and, depending on your role, it can be helpful to share your job title so the customer knows whom they're talking to. A client seeking help will be reassured if you state that you are a product support specialist, for example. Doing so can also knock down skepticism or "Let me talk to your manager" behavior.

Restating the reason for the chat is just another way to personalize the greeting. This might be in the form of acknowledging a problem, such as, "I understand you're having trouble with X, Y, Z," or in setting up the conversation: "I'm looking forward to learning more about your business goals and how our product can help you meet them."

The next phase of the session is getting and keeping you and the customer on the same page. As with all communication, it can sometimes be hard to know what the other person does and doesn't know. It can be even trickier in chat, because you can't hear a hesitation before an answer, or edginess when someone responds to being told something they already know. This is where chunking information becomes extremely important: not only is it the best way to make sure that information is easily digested, it provides opportunities to confirm understanding as you go.

Chunking information is the best way to make sure that information is easily digested. It also provides opportunities to confirm understanding as you go.

As you first see the question or problem, restate your understanding in the moment to ensure that neither of you is making assumptions or jumping to conclusions. Use phrases such as, "Let me check so I have this right" or "So you're saying that . . ." Or restate the issue, adding, "Is that correct?" When you need additional context, ask open-ended questions such as, "Tell me more about this" or "What are you hoping to accomplish?" This gives the chatter a chance to share information that will help you solve the real problem. Just be cautious about asking questions that don't seem to be leading to a solution or an answer. When you don't need clarification, move ahead and impress the customer with your insight and speed.

Sometimes you will have to look something up, consult with a manager or a colleague, transfer a customer to another department, or even just say no. These situations can be either annoying to the client or an opportunity to demonstrate you're working hard on their behalf. Often the difference between the two outcomes is simply communicating well about what needs to happen and then finding the positive in the situation. If you need to research a question or get approvals, ask if it's OK for you to take the time to do so. You'll almost certainly get permission to do so as well as goodwill, because you asked first. But if the answer is no, that allows you to understand the constraints the customer has. You can work out an alternative method for getting the information, such as setting up an appointment or following up via email. When the situation requires something more annoying, such as a transfer or an unpleasant answer, your text will have to work extra hard to create a positive spin.

Use the techniques discussed above to reframe to good news. Don't forget to use *because* in order to reassure the client that you have reasons for your actions and aren't just being lazy or obstinate.

In the event that the client is or becomes angry, remaining in control of the chat becomes even more important. First and foremost, you have the right to expect and ask for civility. If the person is just upset, a firm request for respectful language can sometimes be enough to move forward. Some customers, however, just want to vent and aren't looking for solutions. If the client remains belligerent or rude, or at any point gets foul or personal, execute the ban or end the session procedure immediately. The chat setting can bring out the worst in some people, especially if and when it's anonymous. Make sure your organization's policies allow for this reality and that you have clear escape routes if you end up chatting with a true troll.

◇◇◇

Many agents report that chat support is far less stressful than phone support.

◇◇◇

The good news, however, is that many agents report that chat support is far less stressful than phone support, that it is easier to read difficult language than to be shouted at, and that the format allows time to think and respond stoically, which is a key factor in diffusing anger.

The AAA Method

When customer frustration is real and there is a problem to be solved, you can use the AAA method for diffusing anger with a chat support spin:

Acknowledge the customer's frustration by repeating the problem in your own kind and positive words.

Align with the customer's perspective. In chat, this could literally mean reading between the lines. If someone is angry, for example, that their delivery is delayed in December, you might read between the lines that what they are really upset about is not receiving it before Christmas. This is just another way to show empathy and see the problem from their point of view. They may be worried about not having a gift to give.

Assure the customer that you are there to help them by solving the problem, providing them with information, or, in some cases, making amends. These and other mitigation techniques are familiar to any support agent. When working in chat, however, you'll have to work harder to make your words convey calmness and empathy without having a tone of voice to do that work for you.

The Solutions Phase

Now we move into the solutions phase. With a clear understanding of the question or problem, you can hit the nail on the head with your answer. This is the fun part. Of course you'll get it right, but chat gives you more opportunities than other support venues to confer with colleagues and management. Use this efficiency to your advantage. Build collaborative processes that allow you to get answers behind the scenes from other specialists without having to transfer your client. Once your solution is in place, start chunking and checking in. Keep the customer with you, and confirm that they are still there.

Here's a fun way to think about explaining complicated answers. There's a Subreddit called "Explain It Like I'm Five," which queries experts to explain a complex topic in very simple terms as if they're speaking to a small child. The answers are often brilliant and extremely educational and by no means insulting. Often the answers are perfect for adults who are interested in topics they don't have information about. This approach can be especially helpful if you often have to explain very technical solutions to nontechnical customers.

If you are working on technical products and can try solutions in your own local environment, do so before starting to work through steps with the customer. Follow along as well, so you can adapt if they make a mistake or change what they are asking. Chat is a tool that exists on the same platform many users are working on and asking questions about, so it offers more opportunities to teach clients to solve problems, self-serve, and become more skilled overall.

When at all possible, take advantage of knowledge-base articles that will solve problems as well as providing an ongoing resource for the next time the customer performs the task. Share those links. Also share real screenshots of the solution or real images that illustrate instructions.

If your technology allows, you may also be able to share a screen and coach the user in real time or even take control of the client's computer to perform actions remotely. Be sure, though, that if you use these last two techniques, you clearly communicate what you plan to do and get permission, especially when you are accessing a computer remotely. Be sure the customer is absolutely clear about what is going to happen so they don't panic when cursors and menus start moving on their own. And don't forget to narrate what you are showing. Your clients will be far more likely to perform their task on their own later if you take the time to teach as you go.

Finally, how you end can be just as important as how you begin. This is where you can feel out whether the client is happy, frustrated, worried, or simply on to their task. Make sure you communicate and confirm that the client understands the next steps they need to take. If there is any doubt, give them a way to seek additional help and provide an opportunity for them to ask another question. Allow a beat of silence after asking. (In this context, a beat of silence is metaphorical: a pause before you type your next question.) You may find that your customer speaks up in that gap with something they have previously hesitated to ask.

Finally, depending upon the person, use brief, casual, and personal conversation to leave on a note of warmth and familiarity. Even if it seems obvious or redundant, be sure to clearly state, "I'm logging out now. Goodbye!" so the customer is sure you're ending. Just be aware that the client might not be so considerate. Don't be offended. If a client goes quiet during a session, allow several minutes before you close or pause it. They're multitasking too. They may just need to answer the phone or use a tissue.

Business Writing Skills

With chat support, writing skills are front and center. To illustrate the importance of professional writing, there is the cautionary tale of a man who was tricked into an email scam and ended up chatting with support that he believed was PayPal. Although he had been warned frequently about scam emails, it was the poor grammar and spelling in the supposed support chat that finally aroused his suspicions, and he backed out without harm.

This shows that spelling and grammar are not only professional, they are essential for creating trust. Besides proofing every message for clarity and accuracy before you hit *send*, don't forget to look for those pesky errors that can trip up even the most diligent writer. While chatters are going to be more forgiving than other audiences about small spelling errors, frequent mistakes create and can lose customer trust—and your job will be much easier if the client trusts you. For digging deeper into grammar and style details, you will always of course defer to your organization's required style guides, but what is included below is a very common set of styles—rules of thumb to get you thinking about the kinds of things you'll want to confirm in your own guide.

You'll usually use standard capitalization, which is more formal than texting with family and friends. On the opposite extreme, never use all caps, which is the same as saying, don't shout at your customers. In a friendly chat, you might leave off apostrophes and possessive nouns and contractions, but stick with them in a professional chat. The same with commas, though to save keystrokes, you can opt out of the so-called Oxford comma: in the sentence "Today is warm, cloudy, and humid," the Oxford comma is the one after "cloudy." Use it only when it adds clarity. Also keep in mind that if you are using a lot of commas, you might be making your sentences too complex for a chat setting. Let them be a red flag for you if they come up in anything other than lists.

You'll probably be asked to write complete sentences, not fragments or run-ons (as might be allowed with friends). Do check your style guides, though, as shorter thoughts that might not make full-sentence status but still sound professional are a great technique to master.

This leads us to a broader statement: be concise. You've probably heard the Mark Twain quote: "I apologize for such a long letter; I didn't have time to write a short one." Writing clearly with minimal words is hard. Take time to edit if you can, and practice using the active voice. "Complaints are taken seriously" is passive. Instead, use the active voice and say, "We take complaints seriously." In most cases, the active voice is not only more professional, it's shorter. You may get the best result if you practice starting with how you'd speak your response and then write a slightly more professional version of that. Think of chat messages as dialogue in a novel. You want them to sound like a real person is speaking, but the reader expects professional typesetting and punctuation.

Another crucial point: we may not realize how often we slip into jargon when immersed in an industry or even when we tell ourselves we're being professional. Remember "Explain Like I'm Five" as a standard for clarity. Maybe even jot down a list of jargon words that you find yourself falling into. Avoid acronyms like CTA, ROI, SEO, SEM, and CTR unless you are absolutely certain that they are clear to the client.

If you talk in-house about "accommodating customer requests," you might put that expression on your list. Use "help" or "handle" instead: "I am sure we can help you with that request" instead of, "I am sure we can accommodate your request."

You wouldn't want to type, "Go to page three and click on it or send your contact information to us." You'll say instead, "Click on the 'click here' button." Yes, it's obvious; type it anyway. Help your customer navigate details they might run into and be sure to include all the information they'll need to complete a task, whether while you are watching or sending them off to try on their own.

Recently a nonprofit rolled out a new phone app to all their members. They quickly realized they had to include in all their instructions how to find an input iPhone app store, login, and enter the password to complete the download. Even though those steps weren't remotely related to the app, the organization needed to coach people; otherwise, they would get stuck before they even got to the app.

Precision is important for all business writing. The best way to make sure that you are communicating clearly is to put yourself in the shoes of your reader. What do they know, what do they see, what do they have access to? Pronouns, for example, can get writers into trouble, as we saw in the above example, where a customer support person mistakenly assumed that the client was male. Like writing concisely, writing precisely can take deliberation and practice, but the reward will be satisfied customers and the knowledge that you've truly helped people accomplish their goals.

Key Points in This Chapter

1. Live chat is popular with customers.
2. Chat is different from other forms of communication.
3. Learn how to hone your replies for the chat audience.
4. Learn best practices used by successful agents to ensure a successful support session.
5. Learn common mistakes to avoid.
6. Learn overcoming negativity bias.
7. Learn techniques for guiding a conversation from beginning to end.
8. Learn business writing styles you can tailor to a chat customer experience.

FOUR

Using Inbound Email Strategies

S mall, medium, and large organizations are all similar in that they struggle with managing inbound email, so this chapter will explore this issue.

There are five parts:

1. Inbound email as a critical customer service tool
2. The various elements of a successful inbound email program
3. How to develop great email content
4. Available technology options and how to effectively select and use them
5. Using inbound email to help shape your organization's strategy and future

For our purposes, let's consider inbound email to be email that comes into your organization from external sources, often from existing or potential customers. Inbound email generally refers to single transactional messages. This includes requests for information; sales, service, or support requests; questions about a status, such as when a new product will be released or when an order will be delivered; and complaints. Complaints can be further broken down into complaints about your organization and its processes versus those about a product or service.

The Inbound Email Life Cycle

Dealing with inbound email is a complex problem, so it is helpful to look at it from a life cycle perspective.

1. **Engagement.** This is defined as the set of activities that occur when the person sending you the email is engaging with your organization. This is often through a website, although people may be motivated to send you email based on an in-person transaction or a phone call.

2. **Routing.** This is the set of activities that brings the email into your organization and sends it to the correct person or technological response process.

3. **Response.** This includes the content of the response and also involves matching the correct response to the correct question.

4. **Delivery,** where the response actually gets back to the person who submitted the original email.

5. A **feedback** step, whereby the original writer can provide you feedback about your response you gave or you can invite feedback to see if your response has actually met the need.

This brings us full circle to a new engagement. Each of these steps on its own may sound simple, but when taken together can result in a very complex workflow, with a multitude of processes and roles.

The Inbound Email Life Cycle

1. Engagement
2. Routing
3. Response
4. Delivery
5. Feedback

Converting Interest to Outcomes

Learning from inbound email can help shape the user experience in both online and in-person contexts. It opens a door to real-time feedback, and it can convert interest to outcomes.

An effective email interaction program may increase the proportion of casual visitors who become clients or customers. This directly supports organizational success.

From a big-picture perspective, what are the key success factors for an inbound email program? First, it must advance the mission in measurable ways. You need to know how the program impacts your mission. Second, it is important to demonstrate that your inbound email program is achieving more benefits than costs. Third, your program should follow effective and efficient processes. This is necessary to fulfill the first two success factors.

Finally, the program needs to balance stability and scalability. Stability means that you have a repeatable process that everyone knows how to use. Scalability means that the process can be changed to accommodate more incoming messages as you continue to grow and people discover that mode of communication.

Here are some questions to find the scope of an inbound email program:

- What is the estimated income volume of email?
- What do you predict the nature of the messages will be?
- What level of service do you want to provide? This includes both the timeliness and the depth and quality of responses.
- What is your existing capacity to respond?
- How do you get started?

Start by talking to the people in your company that are getting inbound email, whether you have an inbound email program or not. In the current online environment, people will find you even if you do not formally invite incoming email. Assessing who is already getting incoming messages, as well as the volume and nature of those messages, will help you get a handle on the initial scope.

Costs and Benefits

Let's look at some costs and benefits of an inbound email program. The benefits are that you are better able to retain contacts. You're able to improve the user experience. You are providing increased service, and you have the opportunity to resolve more issues as the result of a first contact.

The primary costs involve labor, whether that is internal or contracted out; technology; and time and effort required for management to administer an inbound email program.

Now let's look at the costs of *not* investing in an inbound email program. Chances are that your organization is already getting inbound email; it just may be happening under the radar. The costs here are inconsistent messaging, as individuals respond to incoming messages on their own; inefficient or slow response rates, given that there's no standard level of service; and inefficiencies introduced by having a lot of duplicate ad hoc emails flying back and forth in and out of the organization.

There's also the problem of the silence of lost customers: customers that come to your website looking for something, can't find it, and go elsewhere without your ever having the chance to help.

Together, all of these factors result in a higher cost of customer acquisition: each customer costs more in time and effort to bring on board than is necessary.

Considerations

Here are the primary areas to consider when initiating an inbound email program. First, you need to determine your goals. Why are you doing this? Next, you need to estimate incoming demand. Again, past experience can inform this answer. You also need to assess your current resources. For example, you may have people who already spend a lot of time doing this, and there may also be a lot of preexisting content that could feed into a formal program. You also need to evaluate the existing content. Have people been informally providing the correct answers? What information would you like to be providing that you don't see in the answers that have been going out?

All of this information can be used to model a future program. Draw out how the inbound email life cycle would play out in your organization. Who are the actors? What are the workflows? What is happening when and how and in a future state? Drawing all this out helps you develop a staged plan.

Starting small is almost always wise when setting up an inbound email program. It is easier to test a pilot program and then build up. It's tempting to launch a state-of-the-art program that you believe will meet all your needs for a long time, but then it becomes very difficult to evaluate and adjust it in a nimble way.

Starting small is almost always wise when setting up an inbound email program.

If you already have an inbound email program, congratulations! Now let's evaluate that program. What's working well? What are the current weaknesses and the impact of those weaknesses based on what's working well and what's not? What do you want to change? Where are these opportunities for change? Finally, are people ready for that change?

Sitting down and walking through those questions should help shape the path ahead.

Now let's move from general success factors to concrete performance measures. Determine the quantitative impact your inbound email program should have on your organizational goals and existing performance targets. Begin with the end in mind. What performance measures at the organizational level is your inbound email program intended to support? Don't do email for the sake of doing email. Know what outcomes you are trying to shape.

Other performance measures may include engagement volume and quality. In fact, your goal may be to *decrease* the amount of email coming into your organization by providing better information upfront. In turn, you want the times when you do need to engage to include the highest-quality information. Possible response time may also be a performance measure. How quickly do you want emails to be responded to?

Finally, and very importantly, consider how you will assess the return on investment. Doing an inbound email program well is going to take some resources. How will you be sure that the investment has either saved money or increased success in measurable ways?

Establishing Effective Workflow

Let's discuss the roles, structures, processes, and workflow that are required to establish an effective inbound email program. We can begin by revisiting the first three steps of the inbound email life cycle that were introduced at the beginning of this chapter: (1) engagement, (2) routing, and (3) response. Let's look at these three steps more closely.

For the engagement step, we are considering the external user experience. How many incoming email boxes do you want to provide? How will you name those boxes so the visitor understands which one to use? Do you want to provide people's names? Some organizations don't want to have impersonal email accounts, like support ads or training ads or sales ads. They would rather have a more personal touch so the visitor understands that a real person will get their message.

On the other hand, using real names can be a problem if that person leaves or multiple people are playing the same role. Some organizations solve this problem by having a generic name to represent the people behind the scenes. For example, the U.S. Department of Agriculture has an "Ask Karen" site. Karen is a virtual representative who answers food safety questions. One company has an "Ask Bob" email. Bob is the founder of the business. People understand that they're not actually going to reach Karen or Bob, but the name is a metaphor for a real-life person.

Let's take a closer look at the question of many or one email boxes. The advantage of having many email boxes is that the customer must really think through the nature of their question in order to pick the right box. Box specialization requires the user to do some thought work. It may also increase confidence, because the user sees that the organization has thought about the boxes that are available and is therefore more likely to monitor them.

The downside of this approach is that customers who aren't sure what box to send their message to may send the same messages to many boxes. Another downside is that the user may just give up because it's not really clear whom to send the message to. (Of course, you could argue that if someone can't decide what email box to send a message to, they probably weren't going to be converted to a customer anyway.)

Now let's look at the pros and cons of having one box. Having a single point of entry for a customer simplifies the experience for them. One choice saves time. The downside of one box is that some customers may be a little wary of boxes like "info at . . ." or some other single generic box, wondering if it will just go into the Internet ether. Nevertheless, having one box makes it easy for someone to send messages without putting much thought into it. As a result, they are more likely to get an email into your system, but that engagement requires little thought and may be of lower quality. Again, a lot of this depends upon your unique organization, the products and services that you provide, and the type of people that visit your website. The point here is to provide you with a structure for thinking about these questions for your own situation.

In general, it's a good idea to have an immediate auto-reply to incoming messages so the sender knows that the email worked. This may be a very simple email reply stating, "Thank you for your message" and perhaps providing some timeline for a response. It may be a reply email with pointers to additional information, which in fact may answer their question. Finally, it may be a reply link to a frequently asked question (FAQ) section of the website (again, perhaps pointing the person to the answer to their question). There are many options, but complete silence is rarely a good idea.

It's a good idea to have an immediate autoreply to incoming messages.

Now let's talk about routing. Regardless of how many email boxes the visitor can choose from, you decide whether you want them all to come into one place or to separate places, depending on the box. For example, one organization has six different boxes, each of which is routed to a different group. Sometimes a group gets a message that doesn't belong to them, and there are established processes for forwarding it to the correct box.

Who is going to monitor these incoming emails, and how often? What processes do you use to sort and triage the messages? How much of all of this can and should be automated? Given your organization, its size, and the types of messages, do you need technology to take the lead in sorting based on program business rules, or is it going to be faster and more effective for a human to do it?

Next we turn to developing the response. This requires understanding the common types of messages you receive. When you think about the possible incoming messages, can you anticipate a target percentage for questions that can be answered with a generic, standard response? For example, you may get many questions that are very personal for the sender but essentially focus on how to complete a certain process. While these questions may come in many variations, the answer may be approximately the same for all of them, and everyone needs to follow essentially the same process regardless of their circumstances. The question here is, can you write a response that covers the vast majority of cases while still allowing any specific visitor to feel that his or her needs were met?

Again, this is driven completely by your organization and what you do. The general questions, however, are the same: Do you want a few broader, more generic answers that can cover more incoming questions? Or is your content more specific, so that you may need to have many standard responses that are specifically focused?

The ability to see patterns across incoming emails is critical in developing an inbound email program. Let's apply a general operational rule of thumb to inbound email. You may know the 80/20 rule, which holds that approximately 80 percent of your results will flow from 20 percent of the work, meaning that 20 percent of the work takes 80 percent of the time. This rule repeatedly plays out with inbound email in many organizations. In general, approximately 80 percent of your messages should be handled with standard responses, while 20 percent will likely need special handling or a customized response. Your goal is always to increase the payoff for lower investment, so get the 80 percent number even higher and the 20 percent number even lower. The best systems require very isolated special handling or customization.

Approximately 80 percent of your messages should be handled with standard responses, while 20 percent will likely need a customized response.

Time, Cost, and Quality

Here's another operational rule of thumb. There are three factors: time, cost, and quality. You can only pick two. You have to sacrifice one variable to get the other two. To get something done very quickly and at a very high quality, you're going to incur a higher cost. To get something at a very low cost, you need to be willing either to spend more time or to sacrifice some quality. It is rare to get something very quickly at a very high quality *and* at a very low cost.

This is a very useful triad in thinking about trade-offs with inbound email. If you respond very quickly using cheap resources, the quality is likely to suffer. On the other hand, developing high-quality responses comes with a cost of more money or more time. You have to balance these three variables in designing your program.

Here are some of the risks that emerge if we do not effectively balance time, quality, and cost variables. There may be too much or too little information provided to the visitor, which leads to frustration. You may spend a lot of time customizing individual messages, leading to too much investment with too little payoff. Too much automation based on keywords may misinterpret the need or concern. Too little emphasis on consistency between staff may cause conflicting information to be sent. Finally, enthusiastic engagement may lead to low follow-ups with lower payoff.

Delivery and Feedback

Now let's turn to the last two steps of the inbound email life cycle: delivery and feedback. Some may wonder why delivery is its own step. You're just pushing *send* on an email, right? In this life cycle model, there's more to it than that. Think about *how* the information will be sent. Are you sending a response email or are you providing a link to web-based content so that you have control over the response in your own infrastructure? Who's the sender of the message? In the world of spam, messages from generic email boxes may go into the spam box of your recipient, defeating the point of leaving the message. Do you want people to be able to reply to the sender's box, or do you indicate that the box does not accept incoming replies? How you send the message communicates whether you encourage follow-up or not.

Also consider how you are going to save and log the response. How do you keep track of what messages go out so you can monitor metrics about the time it took to respond and the number of responses that were sent in any given time period? What follow-up options are you offering? Do you allow the person to reply if they have more questions, do you send them to a different process, or do you stay silent?

This point directly feeds into the final step, which is feedback. Do you track responses to your responses, and if so, how? These responses may be positive, like, "Thank you for replying to my email; that really helped," or corrective: "That's not what I asked at all. What I really need to know is . . ." Also, how do you trace postengagement action by the visitor? For example, if you sell products, you want to know if your email response led to a sale that might not have otherwise been realized.

Finally, you need to decide whether to send a follow-up satisfaction survey. For example, some organizations send an email that says, "We recently answered a question that you submitted online. Did our response get you what you needed?" Many of these surveys may go unanswered, but that query still may have benefits, because it communicates that you care whether your information was useful or not.

Walking through the inbound email life cycle steps provides a structure you can use when designing or evaluating an inbound email program. There are many payoffs from this planning process. Having clear roles, workflows, and processes encourages consistency across the team. It helps you find the right balance between timeliness and the quality of responses. It helps identify ways to measure engagement through inbound email, and it can help you maximize the payoff for your investment in the program.

Developing Effective Content

This section focuses on the language of the messages themselves. First, let's look at the characteristics of effective email content. Effective emails are audience-focused and clearly relevant to the need. The content is written with the end in mind. It focuses on the visitor's needs rather than what the organization wants to say. Effective messages follow a clear structure and are accurate and precise. They are polite but concise. No doubt you've received far too many emails that spend the first paragraph thanking you for your message and telling you how wonderful the organization is. It is preferable to send a message that starts with a thank-you for the inquiry and moves along to what the customer needs. If you do this, the customer will likely think you're wonderful. Finally, your email language should be actionable. It should explain what the next steps are, who takes them, and what the outcome will be.

Here is a five-step model for thinking about content development:

1. List your model questions: the representative questions that result from your planning process. Fifty people will have fifty different ways to ask how to engage in the same process, but here your model question is, "How do I engage in this process?"

2. Identify the existing content that you have that responds to those model questions. This content may live in many places: your website, past emails, instructions, fact sheets, or other resources. Check with people who have frequent visitor contact, and they will likely provide a wealth of information

3. Develop a standard outline for responses. Developing different messages is much easier if you have a standard template outline that can be used as a similar guide for each one. This also supports consistency.

4. Populate your model outline with the content for each response you're going to generate.

5. Engage in review and testing to make sure that the response is accurate and understandable.

Five Steps for Content Development

1. List your model questions.
2. Identify your existing content.
3. Develop a standard outline for responses.
4. Populate your model with content.
5. Engage in review and testing.

Use plain language to respond to inbound email. Plain language is communication that your visitors can both understand and use. Your goal is to increase both the effectiveness of the information and its accountability, so that everyone understands who needs to do what as a result of reading your message.

Plain language generally leads to fewer follow-up questions, saving time for both you and your audience. It allows people to share the knowledge with others so you are not only communicating with the visitor that sent you the message, but with other people that the visitor interacts with in the future.

Plain language realistically and actionably answers practical questions. It answers the actual question asked and anticipates the underlying need. This does not mean customizing for every individual circumstance. People with different stories have shared needs. Your job is to identify the underlying need that applies across several individuals.

Content Governance

When we think about governance, we are often thinking about how organizations run themselves. Governance also works when we are thinking about content. What incoming patterns do we see over time?

Understanding and abstracting patterns allows you to develop new representative questions. Remember the 80/20 rule. Look for patterns across the questions that appear to be outliers. There may be a new category that you missed the first time around. If you are able to group these types of questions, you may be able to build a new standard response that will take care of them.

It's also important to establish an editorial calendar, which will govern when response content is reviewed. There's nothing more frustrating for a visitor than receiving an email with links to helpful information, but half the links are broken.

Establish an editorial calendar, which will govern when response content is reviewed.

A regular editorial review will make sure that you catch updates that need to be cascaded into your response content. This process also includes curating existing responses. For example, you may have received feedback that one of your responses is too general to be useful and that you need to split it into two separate responses to apply more directly to people's needs. On the other hand, you may see a lot of overlap between two categories, so it would be beneficial to join separate responses into one more generic response. This editorial review requires some work but can have a significant impact on the quality of the messages that you send.

Every organization is going to have different needs for content governance, depending on the nature of the industry and the types of incoming messages the company is responding to. Part of content governance is establishing a diverse review team. Here are some examples of the type of people that you might want on this team.

The more complex and technical your content, the more likely you are to need more specialized reviewers. First, there are subject matter experts, who review the technical elements of your message. Communications and marketing individuals will review the message for its theme and tone. A strong writer or editor can make sure the message is written in plain language and that it is grammatically correct and follows the standard format agreed to in the organization. Some messages may require legal review to ensure compliance with rules or policies.

Finally, there should be a leadership sign-off process. Although it may seem odd to have a leader in the organization reviewing someone's email, this email is going to go to a lot of people and is therefore part of your organization's public messaging.

Common Content Problems

Now let's look at some common content problems and their solutions. Paragraphs often hold too many ideas, sentences are too long and too complex, and there are too many strings of texts. Look for lots of commas.

Another common problem is that actors and actions are unclear. For example, an email may say, "It's important that this information be carefully reviewed to ensure compliance." This is an example of the passive voice. It fails to answer the questions of who is doing the review, and in order to be compliant with what? Finally, sometimes we fail to find simpler words.

One common content development challenge is that the content often assumes that the person already knows about the organization. This shows in the use of jargon and acronyms. Once you have identified this problem, try to use simpler, less organizationally specific terms. For example, use "our team" rather than naming a specific division or department. Have someone outside the organization check the message for jargon, acronyms, terms of art, and terms that have very specific meaning for a specific community. It is extraordinarily useful to test your content with outside people.

Here's another challenge. When an organization tries to cover too many scenarios with a single response message, it can lead to content that is too general, making it not actionable enough. The opposite problem can also happen: content that is too specific loses the overall goal or road map to the endpoint.

To address these two risks, tier information into primary information and secondary information. For example, at the top of your message, you could list five key steps for moving forward and then go into more information about each of those steps. Headings and subheadings will help your readers skim to find the specific information they need. Summarizing the key next steps at the end of the message can help the reader synthesize the information appropriately.

Here's a final challenge, which is more technical. Sometimes the marketing team wants to insert visually pleasing or brand-identifying graphics into your message. The message can display improperly, detracting from your content. The recipient may see a lot of boxes with X's in them and has to scroll down to read the actual message. This defeats the purpose. Even with advances in design these days, it is wise for organizations to value substance over style when thinking about email. Keep design simple, minimize graphics, and test your messages with multiple email clients. Not everyone uses Microsoft Outlook or Gmail.

Let's briefly review the best practices introduced above. First, take the time to track trends across your incoming messages. Use those trends to identify new content needs. This requires a regular review schedule, whereby you vigorously curate existing content using diverse review teams. Regular customer testing and feedback can help make sure that your messages are effective. Setting up an inbound email program takes a lot of investment. Effective content governance over time helps to maximize the impact of that investment.

Electronic Management Tips

Now we can turn to the electronic side of inbound email management. The technology of email engagement may take different forms. For example, you may have an email address that the person clicks on, which in turn activates the user's email program to send a message. Alternatively, you may have an online form that the person completes and submits. (In general, we are talking about email here, but online forms work in almost identical ways.)

This brings us to a central question: do you want to handle your inbound email response program using your standard existing business tools, such as your existing email programs and databases, or do you want to invest in specialized software that is developed specifically to manage inbound email? Many specific software tools are designed solely to manage inbound email. Do you want to invest in one of those, or do you want to build upon your preexisting tool set?

To evaluate this decision, let's review the key capabilities that often come with specialized inbound email management software. No tool does everything, and tools for handling inbound email are no different. Inbound email tools generally focus on one or two of three primary capability areas: (1) Customer tracking. These tools often emphasize a customer relationship management component. (2) Handling all the content that goes into the messages that you send. These tools often emphasize a knowledge management component. (3) Focus on the email management process, specifically the triage, routing, and workflow elements of inbound email. These tools often emphasize the workflow component.

When you are looking at software options, consider which of the three categories the software appears to address most centrally. Next, consider the technological factors you need to think through. What is the intended scale and user base of your system? How many licenses will you need, and how much volume do you anticipate? What cost are you willing to incur for a technology system? Technology systems often have two costs: an upfront cost to get it established, and ongoing maintenance and licensing fees. These may be well worth it if it means that you do not have to design your own system, but you need to understand these costs up front.

Finally, there are maintenance and administration require-ments. What kind of technical skills do you need to have on staff to maintain and administer the software? What happens if you want to eventually divest yourself of the software? Will you be able to get your data out of the system to use in another tool?

Using Microsoft Office

Microsoft Office is a popular software suite for both large and small organizations, so let's take some time to review some ways in which it can be used to support inbound email management. Most of these functions are available in other business-oriented software as well, but let's use Outlook as the representative case.

First, shared email boxes are the most straightforward way to engage in an inbound email program. Mail comes into a single box, even if the customer sees several options, and several staff members are able to access the box in order to read and respond to messages. Once these permissions are established (which a savvy email administrator should be able to do), you establish operating rules for what different staff members will do when they get into the box. These rules ensure that somebody doesn't get answered twice and that everybody gets answered at least once.

For example, you may want to set up a rule that if some-one handles an incoming email, they will then move it into a subfolder indicating it has been responded to. Furthermore, the sent message is saved in the "sent" email box as a record. Sometimes organizations have staff put their initials in parentheses after the subject line of the response so they can track who responded to messages without it being obvious to the recipient.

To ensure consistency and responses and save time in drafting emails, the box may have a subfolder of standard responses that anyone with access to the box may use. When a response seems to fit the incoming message, the respondent simply copies and pastes the response into a message back to the incoming email. This allows a degree of customization. The template response can be slightly modified as needed. The email signature function can be used the same way. While many people insert a signature to share their email address and phone number, signatures can also be used to store template email responses. In this case, the user simply hits "reply" to the incoming message and inserts the signature that contains the answer that the person needs.

All of these practices are primarily driven by people rather than by automated software. This can work well for most small and mid-sized organizations. The key is that everyone sharing the box must be very rigorous in how they engage with it, so messages are handled the same way by everyone. It also requires a regular assignment schedule so that the boxes are regularly monitored at the rates and frequency needed to keep up with the incoming messages.

There should also be a schedule for monitoring the spam folder. Sometimes this can be a good task for an intern, who can, for example, go into the spam folder every other day to skim through the messages and move any real messages into the inbox. Over time, the intern may even become adept at matching template responses to incoming standard questions, leaving only outlier or complicated questions for the paid staff to resolve.

⬦⬦⬦

There should be a schedule for managing the spam folder.

⬦⬦⬦

Outlook has fairly sophisticated message routing and rules. For example, you can set up rules so that if an incoming message contains certain keywords, it can be forwarded to a specific person or moved to a subfolder. You can also set up rules so that an incoming email with a particular address—say all emails with a GoTo extension—are routed to another email or to a subfolder. Many people have emails from their boss go into a specific folder so that they can see them right away. This is the same principle, applied to inbound email.

Outlook also has autoresponses, so you can immediately acknowledge incoming email. Using the "out-of-office" function in Outlook, you can simply tailor your message to acknowledge the incoming message, rather than indicating that someone is out of the office. Microsoft Office tools are very, very flexible. You may use an "out-of-office" message for when you are on vacation, but when applied to inbound email management, it becomes a very easy to use an automated response program.

Other tools in Microsoft Outlook that can be helpful in inbound email management include keyword searches, so you can find messages with similar topics and easily convert emails to tasks or meeting announcements or quickly handle incoming emails that need specialized or individualized attention. Emails that need more attention can be assigned to specific individuals.

Other Microsoft Office tools can be very helpful in inbound email management. Many organizations, for example, use Access or Excel to track content and engagement numbers over time.

Considering how to use specific tools like the Microsoft Office Suite can help you visualize what it will take to set up an inbound email program in your organization.

Once you figure out the rules structure and workflow of your inbound email program, you may be able to extrapolate those approaches to other forms of electronically mediated communication—for example, your social media strategy. Many times, email responses can feed into tweets on X or Meta posts or comments on your organization's LinkedIn page.

If you are interested in extending those tools, you'll want to complete the same planning process you did for email. In general, plan for faster turnaround times, higher engagement, and more public exchanges. The reverse is also true: if your organization engages in a social media strategy before tackling inbound email, that strategy may inform how you address incoming email.

When thinking about using technology to support your inbound email program, remember that technology is always personal. Think about the functions and features of software that are actually needed and valued by the people that will be using that software. Consider the customization that would be required for your staff to use the software, and finally, think through what it will take to maintain. Technology maintenance is also an important part of governance. Remember that software vendors will do a very good job of telling you how great their tool is. Weigh all technology options in the context of your unique culture.

Using Email to Shape Strategy

Organizations that think of inbound email as a mere hassle lose valuable opportunities to shape the organization and its strategy. This section focuses on how to use inbound email in a broader organization development context. Paying attention to themes and patterns in inbound email can point to new strategic goals as well as new services or products that are needed by your visitors. It can provide valuable feedback for improved communication and outreach with your visitors. It can also be a starting point for customer relationship management with valuable prospects.

Finally, your inbound email program can become an essential element of your staff training and development program.

First, how do you use email to shape strategy? Trends and questions, needs and complaints can point to new opportunities and areas of unmet demand. Engaging with visitors and customers that have sent you email offers you the opportunity to learn more about how they are using your products and services and what other needs you may be able to fill. Sometimes incoming email will give you valuable insights into your marketing and messaging strategy. Perhaps people are using your product for something entirely different than you originally intended. You may want to refer to that use in your marketing materials.

Finally, while complaints can be difficult to hear, they are valuable in pointing out problems that you may be blind to. They can also provide data about possible operational weaknesses that you need to explore.

One example: a woman recently bought a pair of shoes online from a company she had always engaged with at a brick-and-mortar store. She had to set up an account indicating she was a new online customer. Within an hour of submitting the order, she received two emails encouraging her to order even more shoes before midnight that night.

The woman responded by noting that this kind of email campaign might be more effective if they waited until she actually received her order, particularly since this was the first time she'd ordered online from this firm. She got an automated response to her email within three minutes, pointing her to a web page where she could track her order and to another page with even more coupons to use before midnight.

The customer was trying to provide operational feedback that she thought might be useful, but she doubts that her message ever found a human being. Objectively, the organization lost little from that transaction. She liked the shoes when they arrived and will probably order again. However, the organization might have learned something through that interaction. Of course, that would have taken time and a different process for dealing with email. Every organization must decide for themselves what those trade-offs are.

Inbound email can play a valuable role in shaping your online content. If you get a lot of questions about a specific

topic, consider adding that topic to a frequently asked questions (FAQ) page. You can also consider redesigning your
website to put the information that is most often requested
on the front page. If you take care of the information needed
upfront, the amount of inbound email may drop, or the nature
of the messages may change.

Interactions with visitors and customers can help inform
social media content as well. If people have many questions
about a specific topic, you might consider a regular tweet,
Meta post, or LinkedIn message to hit people who have the
same question but did not send you an email.

Email interactions with visitors and customers can help inform social media content.

Once in a while, engagements with a customer over email
can lead to an interesting ongoing exchange and a productive
ability to learn about a person using your product or service.
If the person is open to it, that customer could become a
highlight for a customer profile or might be willing to share
a quote for your website. Again, if you view incoming email
for its positive potential rather than as an operational hassle,
you can see these opportunities in a different light than you
might otherwise.

Inbound email can also support employee development.
In addition to responding to specific visitors, your inbound
email program is building a comprehensive library of valu-

able information about your organization. This content can become an important part of your onboarding and training programs, particularly if you are cross-training across a complex organization.

This onboarding and training can come in two forms. First, you're teaching technical content, so people better understand your business. Second, you're teaching customer service skills as you show employees how to communicate with visitors and customers through email. This sets an important cultural tone. Customers are important. Integrating content from your inbound email program encourages consistency and cross-organizational understanding.

Building Customer Relationships

Now let's talk about building customer relationships. Effective online encounters can be translated into success stories and loyal customers. People who have engaged with you positively by email will be more likely to subscribe to your newsletters and other online transmissions. This builds your online relationship with them over time. As noted above, you may be able to recruit customers as validators: people who are willing to speak positively and publicly about your organization.

You may also be able to recruit people for reciprocal marketing. What does this mean? If you have a customer who is able to articulate how your organization helped them meet their goals, you could highlight them in a profile. The profile highlights your business, but it also highlights theirs. This kind of engagement is a much more customized and personal level of engagement than that of the shoe company mentioned above. Inbound email will vary an enormous amount depending on your organization, its goals, and its strategy.

The content governance element of your inbound email program can also be used to inform organizational strategy. Review your current materials occasionally for both strengths and gaps. Ask yourself what a new response might look like in one year, based on organizational goals. Are you launching a new service area or considering a new product? Ask yourself what questions your prospective customers would likely ask about your service or product. This can provide valuable insights into your planning processes, beginning with the end in mind. What will people need from us one, two, or three years after we launch this new initiative? This thought exercise can help bridge the strategic with the tactical in a very practical way. Brainstorm the ideal customer experience, and you may be able to identify the steps that will make that vision a reality.

Using Metrics to Assess Success

Let's talk about how to use metrics to assess success. Compare before and after metrics to assess your initial launch. Then monitor trends over time using your organization's success criteria. Finally, evolve your tracking to map engagement so that you can track customer contact to action.

Key Points in This Chapter

1. Inbound email is a critical customer service tool.

2. Email engagement can have a direct and positive impact on your organizational goals.

3. An inbound email program can help you recruit new customers and translate prospects into stakeholders.

4. Inbound email management can help resolve problems faster and with lower staff investment.

5. Customer response and interaction is a major benefit of incoming email.

6. Make sure that the benefits of your inbound email program outweigh the investments in labor, time, and costs.

7. Weigh software options carefully according to your company's specific needs.

FIVE

Leading Your Customer Service Team

We'll now discuss leading and empowering your customer service team. In this chapter, we'll talk about:

1. Identifying common ground with your customer.
2. Methods for leading and encouraging your team.
3. Focusing on solutions, not problems.
4. Moving your team to extraordinary customer service.
5. Responding positively as a team leader even when the stress is building.

Identify Common Ground with the Customer

Once a customer service rep came into his manager's office, threw up his arms in disgust, and said, "Who are these people?"

Most of us feel that way at some point or another. Who are these customers? Where are they getting their crazy ideas? How do you stay calm while dealing with them? Customer service leaders may feel that way about their employees as well. Some days we want to throw up our arms and say, "Who are these people?" We want to just give up and shake it all off.

How do you encourage your team? How do you deal with the difficult customer? How do you aim for common ground in a difficult situation?

The first question we need to ask when we're dealing with customers: is conflict inevitable? Yes, it is. Conflict is absolutely inevitable. As a team leader, you need to make sure you understand that; that will be your reality. You also want to communicate that fact with your team. As you're leading and empowering a customer service team, make sure everyone understands that conflict is inevitable.

Conflict is inevitable.

How, then, do you move past the conflict? How do you move past the unhappy or angry customer to give exceptional customer service?

We've already covered some of these points in discussing customer service representatives, but they also apply to managers and are worth reviewing here.

Remember, your goal is to identify common ground with a customer. One of the best ways to do that is to listen. Sometimes the customer just needs to vent and express their opinion. The best thing we can do in that case is to actively listen. The key phrase to use is, "I hear what you are saying." When you say this, you are not agreeing; you are not disagreeing; you are simply stating that you are listening.

One of the quickest ways to find common ground with the customer is to agree with them. The first question to ask is, "Do I agree?"

Another key statement is, "I can understand why you feel that way." This is similar to "I hear what you are saying" but goes one step further. Once again, your goal is to make sure the customer knows that you are listening.

◇◇

One key statement:
"I can understand why you feel that way."

◇◇

You also want to be aware of your environment. What message are you sending to your customer apart from your words? First of all, watch your body language. Simple things like crossing your arms or standing towering above the customer sends a loud signal. Watch your body language.

Also watch your tone. Avoid an angry or condescending voice. If you have a sarcastic bent, avoid sarcasm when responding to the customer.

Remove any physical barriers, if possible. Obviously if you're behind a customer service desk, that's the position you need to stay in. But if possible, move and stand beside your customer, especially if you feel their anger is starting to escalate. Try to remove any physical barriers between the two of you. This gives the customer more of a sense that you are open to their suggestions and are listening to their complaints.

As you're moving forward, find common ground with the customer. Make sure you clarify the situation along the way. Here are three easy steps to do so:

1. Repeat what the customer said to you, and say these key words: "Let me repeat what I have heard so far."

2. Paraphrase your understanding back to the customer. If it is not correct, continue to question and converse with your customer until you understand their situation.

3. Agree on the stated problem. That doesn't mean agreeing on a solution yet. You just want to make sure you have a clear understanding of the problem the customer seems to be having.

The Leader's Role

Now let's tie together the advice we've given so far in relation to your role as a leader. Sometimes a customer will not give up until they speak to a manager. Your team players can say the exact same words you would say, they can perform the same actions you would perform, and they can give the same service you would give. However, sometimes customers just want to speak to a manager. As you lead and empower your team members, make that fact clear to them.

To take that idea a little bit further, you can perform the same exact steps and get a different result. In such cases, make sure that your team realizes they have done nothing wrong. Communicate that even though you take the same steps, you will get a different result simply because your title is that of team leader or manager.

As you're focusing on finding common ground with the customer, awareness of your role as the manager is critically important from the point of view of both the customer and your team. Your goal as the team leader is to have both a satisfied customer and a satisfied team. Training and hiring are extremely expensive. While your main goal is a satisfied customer, you achieve that end by having a satisfied team. A satisfied customer comes from having a satisfied customer service team.

Here are some questions to consider as you're moving toward a solution with your customer:

- Is it reasonable? Is this a reasonable compromise?
- Is my company OK with this solution?
- Is this within my authority?
- How do I make this customer happy?
- How do I provide extraordinary customer service?
- Is the compromise I'm proposing within my authority?
- Finally, what precedent will this set? I want to make sure I make my customer happy. However, I also need to make sure I don't go too far above the limits of what my company will allow, because once I do this action for one customer, I will be asked to take the same action for other customers in the future.

Two questions you need to ask as you're proposing a compromise:

- How much can I compromise to make this customer happy?

That answer usually comes from company policy. The next question is just as important:

- How much should I compromise to make this customer happy?

Let's tie these considerations together. We've discussed how much you can compromise and the precedent this will set for future customers. Let's take the next step: ensure that your team is empowered to make these same compromises. Make sure they know what the precedent is, make sure to communicate with your team so they can start leading themselves.

Our goal as we lead and empower our customer service team is to aim for common ground with the customer. Then take that next step: communicate the precedents and the compromises you can make so that your customer service team has the authority and power to find common ground.

Encouraging Your Team

As a leader, how do you encourage your team? An important goal is to make sure customer service representatives know their strengths. You can start by asking everyone on your team to write down their number one strength. You can go a couple of ways with this: you can ask them to write down their number one strength without parameters, you can ask them to write their number one strength as a customer service rep, or you can do both. Then ask your team to share their number one strength. They can share it with one other person in the room or out loud. It's totally up to you as the leader.

The main reason for this strengths activity is that the loudest voice in your ears is your own. Yes, you want your team to share their strengths with you and with others. But the most important person to hear the number one strength is that individual.

◇◇

The loudest voice in your ears is your own.

◇◇

Let's talk about awareness levels with our team. Ask what actions sends them over the edge; then ask, "What can I, as your team leader, do to help beforehand, before this situation comes up?"

Then ask what you can do to help *during* the situation. Leaders, when your customers are encountering an angry customer or a difficult situation, make sure that you, or someone on the management staff, is available to help. Yes, it is our goal to lead and empower, but we need to make sure we are there for our team, especially when someone is in a situation that they know upsets them.

Work with your team players and have them visualize how they will handle that difficult situation in the future. Have them play that movie in their head. Ask them to close their eyes, if necessary, and see themselves handling the situation differently in the future. Then ask them to share that with you. How will they mentally walk away from that situation from now on? As a leader, you can help move team players forward by having them think through a volatile solution before they're in the middle of it.

It's also important to know which actions send each of your team players over the edge. What aggravates one person may not bother someone else at all. If you are aware of that fact, you may be able to shift functions and duties around to prevent team players from encountering the situations that upset them.

Make sure you know the differences between your team players. Understand what actions you should take and what duties and responsibilities each person on your team should have to minimize those situations.

An important part of leading a customer service team is to continually provide stress management training for employees, especially frontline employees, who have an extremely difficult job. Some customers have no other objective than to make the service rep cry, even when they are doing everything right.

Provide constant stress management training for employees. One manager who led a large customer service team explained how her office has an open-door policy for laughter. She—and everyone on her team—knows that after a particularly rough encounter with a customer, they are more than welcome to come to her office and just find something to laugh about and shake the experience off. Of course, you can't allow your team to come back to your office every single time they deal with a customer. But this manager made it clear that after a particularly rough encounter or volatile customer, her employees were more than welcome to come to her office. She helped them work through that so that they would not be upset and take the feeling home.

Model the behavior that you want. Be an encourager. When you see someone on your team doing a good job, tell them, encourage them, give them a reward when possible. When you model that behavior, it's contagious. Others on your team will start encouraging their teammates, modeling the behavior that you want. As the leader, you set the tone, and you set the pace. Your team players are constantly watching you as you interact with customers, so find common ground with customers. When you do it well, they will follow your lead.

◇◇◇

Model the behavior that you want to encourage.

◇◇◇

As you're modeling the behavior that you want to encourage your team to follow, ask yourself this question: "What am I going to say when I'm wrong?" Are you going to mess up? Yes, of course. When you mess up, when you're wrong, say, "I was wrong. Here's what I'll do to take care of that problem next time. I plan to take these steps in order to avoid the situation in the future." As we're encouraging our team, we're building trust and respect. That's one of your goals as a leader.

Similarly, admit when you don't know the answer to a question or a problem. Often we think admitting we don't know the answer makes us look weak or unprofessional, but it builds trust and respect amongst team players. You can't know the answer to everything. When you don't, admit it: "I don't know; I will find out and get back to you."

Admit when you don't know the answer.

Handling Unacceptable Behavior

You'll also define the limits for your team, for example, the limit of unacceptable customer behavior. Make sure that everyone on your team understands the point at which a customer has crossed a particular line and the behavior has become unacceptable. Make sure your team knows that limit, and make sure they have permission to walk away when that line has been crossed. The safety of your team has to come first. Make sure they understand when they can walk away, and help them with that.

Make sure they're trained on what procedures to take. If they feel unsafe or threatened, what should they do? Are they allowed to leave the situation? Are they supposed to call security? Should they come and find you or another manager? Make sure employees are trained on the procedures for unacceptable customer behavior. Constantly encourage employees to take care of themselves first. What can you do to help them with their stress level? What can you do to encourage them?

In addition to encouraging your team, you also want to empower them, especially if you are leading smart, well-defined, well-functioning teams. Empower them to make decisions; give them ownership of as many facets of the project and of as many decisions regarding the customer as possible. One great by-product of empowering your team is that you're shaping future managers. Great leaders create great leaders. Do everything you can to empower your team.

Turning Problems into Solutions

Next, we're going to talk about solutions versus problems. You want to focus your team on the solution, not the problem. Your role as a customer service leader is to focus your team on solutions. Nevertheless, it's common to have at least one employee who keeps focusing on the problem.

To restate a point we've already made: Is it OK to vent? Yes, we all need to vent occasionally. As leaders, make sure you understand that it's OK for your employees to vent. Everyone needs to blow off steam occasionally. But it's important to set limits. You may, for example, let employees vent for about sixty or ninety seconds (or longer if necessary; it's totally up to you). Then your job as a leader is to start reeling them in and focusing them on the solution.

One way to move employees towards a solution is to remind them that they have the best ideas. Where do leaders get their best ideas? From employees. They are doing the job every day. They know the best ways to solve the problem. One way to focus an employee on the solution is to remind them of that fact. Now get them to open up and share those ideas with you.

Your employees have the best ideas.

Brainstorming

Your role is to lead your team towards solution building. How do you do that? Let's look at a few ideas.

Brainstorming is always a great way to focus a team on a solution. Brainstorming is getting your team together and throwing out ideas. During a brainstorming session, no idea is ignored or rejected. All ideas are written down and recorded for later discussion. The beauty of a brainstorming session is that when one person throws out an idea, it will spark ideas from others. The more we throw out and talk about ideas, the more creativity our team displays, leading us to more solutions.

You may have tried a brainstorming session with your team, but it was a failure: if you have a brainstorming session and no one speaks, that is not a success. Or you may have just read this description of a brainstorming session and realized that it will not work with your team. In that case, try brainwriting.

Brainwriting is an offshoot of brainstorming, but it's done in a different environment. Write down the problem, then ask each employee to write a solution on a piece of paper and hand it to the next person. This person will read the problem and the first person's solution, which may spark ideas; then they write down a different problem. At the end of the day, pass those pieces of paper around and ask that each piece of paper have at least three, hopefully five, different solutions for employees to walk away with.

Another way to focus on solutions is to ask *why*. Start with *why* and keep going until you get to the root cause of the problem. This is a great activity to use for recurring problems.

Here's an example everyone can relate to: "My car won't start." The first *why* is, "Because the battery is dead." Then you want to ask yourself, "Why is the battery dead?" Because the alternator is not functioning properly. Why is that happening? "The alternator belt is broken." Why is the alternator belt broken? "Because it was beyond its useful life, and it broke." Why did that happen? "Because the vehicle was not maintained." The real answer, the real *why*, is, "My car won't start because it was not maintained properly." Take this example, and use it in your work situation. Ask *why* until you get to the root of the problem.

Another method to help focus on solutions rather than problems: Try assigning a different hat to everyone. For example, you may assign the first person on your team the task of focusing on the data, the facts. Assign a different hat to the next person: "Your job will be to think creatively; bring every idea you can think of." Then you might ask the third person to wear the hat of intuition. What is their gut feeling on how we should solve this problem? Maybe the fourth person will be your data analyst. They will bring the facts and the figures; they will be the person who brings the twenty-page spreadsheet. Think about your situation, the problem you're having, and assign a different hat to everyone on your team.

Yet another way to help a team focus on the solution instead of the problem is to flip the coin: "What happens if I *don't* focus my team towards solutions?" You can visualize that already: you talk about the problems during meetings and during breaks. While you're working, you focus only on customer problems.

You may have a team member who constantly answers questions with, "I don't know." You're trying to empower and lead them, but their constant answer is, "I don't know." That's frustrating, but here's one approach: when they tell you they don't know the answer, sit back, take a deep breath, and ask the following question: "Well, if you *did* know the answer, what would it be?"

You'll be amazed at the response. For some reason, that additional question will allow the employee to open up and give an answer. At that point, your job is to sit back and listen.

An extremely effective way to help a customer service team focus on the solution is to ask them to put themselves in the customer's shoes. Sometimes obvious answers are overlooked. We think a simple answer will not be good enough for our customers. Turn that around. Ask your customer service team to put themselves in the customer's shoes. What would they want in this situation? What would they want if they encountered this particular problem? As a leader, encourage your team to be proactive. We've already established that the best ideas and suggestions come from team players. Encourage them to be constantly looking forward.

Another idea for leading and empowering your team towards solution building: have a customer on your focus group team. Along with your group of customer service representatives, actually have an outside customer who has been invited to be part of team meetings, especially brainstorming sessions. You may be amazed at how simple solutions from your sample customer will satisfy many in your customer base. Is that something you're able to do in your environment? If so, seriously consider getting a customer on your team—not hiring that person, but asking them to come in as a consultant.

<<<<<<<<<<<<<<<<<<<<<<<<<<<<<<<<<<<<<<<<<<<<<<<<<<<<<<<<<<<<

Have a customer on your focus group team.

<<<<<<<<<<<<<<<<<<<<<<<<<<<<<<<<<<<<<<<<<<<<<<<<<<<<<<<<<<<<

Moving to Extraordinary Customer Service

Let's now talk about moving your team to extraordinary customer service. One of the first steps to take is to have the right person in the right seat. Take the example of an electronics store. When you walk into an electronics store and want to buy a new computer, projector, or speaker system, you want to make sure the person who's taking care of you knows about those products. When you move over into the appliance section, you need someone in that section who knows appliances. Consequently, step one in achieving extraordinary customer service is to have the right person in the right seat.

We've already established that most of our best ideas come from our team. Encourage your team to come up with crazy ideas. You can use brainstorming or brainwriting session to do this. Encourage them to come up with the craziest ideas possible. Put themselves in the customer's shoes. What would they want in any given situation? Listen to every idea put on the table. Set up the brainstorming session by encouraging your team to come up with crazy ideas and then leave the room. If you stay in the room, your team will constantly look to you as the leader for the answers.

Your team members know the best answers, so in order to empower them, give them the proper tools, set up the correct environment, encourage and empower them, and then leave so that they can be honest in coming up with their own ideas.

Of course, you have to come back after a certain period of time. When you do, having empowered your team to share crazy ideas and come up with brilliant solutions, your job at that point is to listen, evaluate, and talk with your team on how to move forward to get the best possible solutions for extraordinary customer service. Constantly encourage your team to think outside the box; bring out the extraordinary in them; guide them in coming up with unique solutions to complex problems.

Thinking outside the Box

As we've already seen, a big part of that process is to make sure you have the right people with the right skill sets on your team. Utilize that advantage during brainstorming sessions to allow the entire team to think outside the box. Here are few ways to help your team with that process:

Shake up the environment occasionally. Have a team session outside, at the beach, or in the mountains, if you live in those areas. Of course, you need to make sure that company policy allows that kind of flexibility. But you're asking your team to be creative; you're asking them to provide extraordinary customer service. Your job is to provide extraordinary resources for them.

Bring in outside encouragement when necessary. Often, especially on long-term projects, teams can get stuck in the details. Take a step back as the leader of the team; bring in some outside encouragement. Bring in an outside coach—someone who can help you evaluate where you are, what your vision is, and where you need to be.

Employees really deliver extraordinary service. They really do. Your job is to constantly build self-esteem. If you can't do that personally, make sure your team has the resources and the mutual encouragement to build their own self-esteem.

Your job is also to lead by example. Make sure you're an extraordinary leader. Think constantly about what you need to do to be an extraordinary leader, because extraordinary employees deliver extraordinary customer service.

One way to keep extraordinary employees is to reward them often. Ask what they want as a reward. Answers will range from money, gift cards, food, and chocolate to a day off. But most likely, the number one answer you will get is acknowledgment—recognition. Employees want to know that you notice. Make sure you reward your employees often.

Reward your employees often.

Turning Vision into Action

Up to now we've talked about ways of getting ideas. Now your job as a leader is to turn those visions into actions. Answers on how to make that happen will vary tremendously. Maybe you want to write down your ideas and send them out to your team. Maybe you want to get them together to write down ideas. In any case, the next step is to turn visions of extraordinary customer service into action items for your team.

How will you know if extraordinary customer service is being given? How will you know if expectations are being met? Social media is a great tool for determining whether your company is providing extraordinary customer service. Make sure that you or someone on your team is aware of social media conversations about your organization.

Another way you can know if the expectations are being met: you will see less stress in employees. When their stress level is lower, when you are there to support them and provide training on stress management, employees will stay longer and will naturally provide extraordinary customer service. That will certainly affect the bottom line. If extraordinary customer service is being given, the bottom line will show it within a certain amount of time.

As a leader, what can you allow and implement for my corporation, for your team, for your company? Can you do the unexpected? Can you go far above and beyond your customers' expectations? When you do, your extraordinary customer service will be talked about on social media.

<<<<<<<<<<<<<<<<<<<<<<<<<<<<<<<<<<<<<<<<<<<<<<<<<<<<<<<

Can you do the unexpected?

<<<<<<<<<<<<<<<<<<<<<<<<<<<<<<<<<<<<<<<<<<<<<<<<<<<<<<<

Leaders think about what they can do to go above and beyond in order to provide extraordinary customer service. You want to build a culture of extraordinary service at your organization, and this will require a different answer for every team. Lead the way at your organization. Stop thinking within your own box, get upper management support, and set the bar higher.

Positive Reaction in Times of Stress

When we're dealing with an angry customer and our stress level is building, the first impulse is to yell and scream in response. Don't do it. Take control of your emotions. Take a deep breath, and count to ten, which will allow you to listen to the customer.

You've heard this before: take a deep breath; count to ten. Does that really work? Yes, it does. Especially in a stressful situation, where your stress level is building and you're trying to control your emotions, it's important to respond positively. Take that step back; take a deep breath; count to ten. Take time to get composed before responding.

Go to work each day with a positive attitude. We set the tone for our environment and our entire team. If you come to work looking for good, you will find it. When you look for bad, it will find you. If you're walking into work announcing that you're expecting to deal with problem customers, then more than likely all day you will deal with problem customers.

Turn that around. As you come in in the morning, realize you do have to deal with difficult customers: that is part of your job. But turn your focus in a different direction: "I will be dealing with difficult customers today, and I'm looking forward to finding effective solutions for their problems. I need to show my team that I can handle almost any situation." We've already seen the need to model the behavior that we want to see in our customer service team. Constantly focus on controlling your emotions, even though you may feel as if a volcano is erupting inside of you and you want to yell and scream. Although you may not want to respond positively at this point, it's imperative to control your emotions and behavior. The customer is not the only one watching your behavior: your team is watching as well. Keeping your stress level low will empower and encourage your staff to do the same as they're dealing with difficult customers too.

You may ask, "Can I totally eliminate stress?" No, you can't, and you don't want to. We do need some levels of stress in our lives. If your building catches on fire, you need to be stressed enough to exit. To relate this principle to responding positively to your customer, think about your safety and that of your employees. If you feel a volatile situation is getting ready to erupt, you want to have enough stress to get away from that situation.

We need some level of stress in our lives.

We can't totally eliminate stress, and we don't want to. Even though you can't totally eliminate stress from your life, you can minimize your stress level. One way to do that is to put yourself first. Although that sounds a bit selfish, you want to put yourself first so that you can be an effective leader; modeling the behavior that you want your employees to see.

Let's go over some ways to keep your stress level low. A few ideas:

Take breaks often. Get away from the hustle and bustle and volatile situations. Walk outside, get a breath of fresh air, even if you walk down the hallway to the water fountain and back. Take breaks often, and make sure your employees are also taking breaks often and scheduling time for themselves. Take lunch, take a vacation. It doesn't have to be a fancy vacation. It can be one where you stay at home and rest. Make sure to schedule time for yourself. Find ways to laugh, especially with your team. Laughter truly is the best medicine.

Take a moment and think about your favorite destressing activity. It could be exercise, a massage, a movie, a nice dinner at a nice restaurant. When was the last time you did that activity?

We're talking about responding positively, even when the stress level is building. Are we going to make mistakes? Yes.

Are we going to fail? Absolutely. When it happens, always remind yourself, "I'm going to fail just like everyone else. Failure is a part of life. I'm going to turn that into a positive experience. What can I learn from the failure? What did we do right during this project? What did I do well during this encounter? What can I take from the experience and move forward?"

Share Your Knowledge

Take this to the next step: share that knowledge with your team. Let them learn from your mistakes and one another's. Sometimes you just have to let go. Let go and accept that there are some things you can't control. You can't control the weather; you can't control traffic. Some days you can't control the person in front of you. Accepting that fact, realizing it, preparing for it in advance will help you keep your stress level to a minimum. It will also help you respond positively to your customer and your team. Maybe you've just had an encounter with a totally disgruntled employee and have had to accept the fact that no matter what you do, you cannot make this person happy. Remember these ideas: "I was chosen for this position. I'm unique and gifted and qualified. Upper management chose me to lead and empower this customer service team. They have confidence in me, and I am a good role model. Everything can't go perfectly all the time, but I am a good role model for my team."

Plan ahead for potential situations that will increase stress levels. Planning ahead allows us to respond positively. What are you going to do with a violent customer? Make sure you know company policy on this subject. If the safety of you or anyone on your team is threatened, what should you do? What does company policy state for this situation?

What should you do when you have two or three angry customers at the same time? Strong hint for you: separate them from one another. Angry customers tend to feed off of each other, so plan ahead: how can you get unhappy customers into separate locations? How can you make that happen? You also want to plan ahead for verbal abuse to your team. This person isn't violent, and your safety is not threatened, but make sure you draw the line, and plan ahead. What will I do when a customer is verbally abusive to me or to anyone on my team?

Here's an important item to keep in mind at all times, and it's one that has been emphasized more than once in this book: *don't take it personally*. Sometimes when we have a violent or disgruntled customer, we've done everything in our power to make them happy, but they're still disgruntled. Don't take that personally. It's not that they don't like you; they don't like themselves.

A final note: remember the only person who can make you unhappy is you. Do other people try? Yes, absolutely, especially in the customer service industry; people may try sometimes on a daily, maybe even an hourly basis. However, the only person who can make you unhappy is you. Share this idea often with your team. Bring it up at meetings. Post it in the break room. You need to be reminded often that you're the only person who can make you unhappy. Sometimes people have a goal to make those around them unhappy, whether it's at work, at the mall, or on the interstate. Don't let them meet their goal. The only person who can make you unhappy is you.

Key Points in This Chapter

1. Encourage your team to look at their strengths.
2. Build trust and respect.
3. Focus on the solution, not the problem.
4. The best ideas often come from team members.
5. Encourage employees to focus on the solution instead of the problem.
6. Use techniques such as brainstorming, brainwriting, and wearing a different hat.
7. Shake up the environment occasionally; allow your employees to get out of their normal surroundings.
8. Reward employees as often as possible.
9. Respond positively, even when the stress level is building.
10. Take care of yourself. Keep your stress level low; take breaks; allow and encourage laughter.
11. Remember: the only person who can make you unhappy is you.

CONCLUSION

We've covered quite a bit of ground in this book. We started with one key point: the customer service representative is the most important person in your company. That employee is your interface with customers and potential customers. The way that individual behaves, responds, and manages customers—no matter how difficult— is the face of your company.

That's why it's so important that customer service reps are trained to have the best and most effective skills.

As we've seen, the first step is learning how to manage emotions. Difficult customers are just a part of the business. Learning how not to react to provocation and retaining a calm and professional demeanor at all times are essential to the best possible responses. That includes not only *what* is said, but *how*. Facial expressions, open body positions, and tones of voice are at least as crucial to your response as the words that come out of your mouth.

Customer service reps—and indeed everyone in your company—need to have a clear sense of what they can and can't control. They may well have no direct input on product quality or timeliness of delivery, but they can behave in respectful and confident ways, no matter what issues may be confronting them. Sometimes an apology is all a customer wants.

Current technology has greatly expanded the possibilities for communicating with customers. One of the most valuable is live chat, whereby a company representative interacts with customers in real time using online text messages. Live chat offers faster resolutions with a lower investment of company time.

Like all forms of communication, live chat has its own unique (though usually unstated) rules of etiquette—going down to timing of responses and even punctuation. Knowing these details is essential to customer satisfaction.

While technology has changed many rules of the workplace, some remain the same as ever. Correct grammar and punctuation—even in short communications—are vital for conveying an image of competence and professionalism. So is avoiding jargon that the recipient may not understand. Again, emotional control is crucial: think (at least) twice before hitting the send button for a strongly worded text or email.

As valuable as live chat is, it doesn't replace email, which in many respects remains the backbone of your communications with customers. Essential to effective email management is organization: making sure that each inbound message is routed to the right employee or department.

But email has more uses than that. Frequent responses and complaints are key indicators of items that your company may need to fix, or add to, your product line. Like live chat, email is superb for building long-term customer relationships and giving you important feedback for shaping strategy.

Chapter 5 discussed managing a customer service team. Many of the principles for dealing with actual customers apply here, such as focusing on solutions rather than problems and maintaining a positive response even when stress is building.

Effective customer communication is not an arcane skill, but it does require knowing the basics and internalizing them so that you—and everyone in your company—can provide the best possible response in every situation.

www.ingramcontent.com/pod-product-compliance
Lightning Source LLC
Chambersburg PA
CBHW071646210326
41597CB00017B/2129